Hat Book

written and illustrated by
Alan Couldridge

General Editor:
Charlotte Parry-Crooke

Knitting Section: Celia Dowell
Photography: David Bradfield

A SPECTRUM BOOK

Prentice-Hall, Inc., Englewood Cliffs, New Jersey 07632

Acknowledgements

The author and publishers gratefully acknowledge the invaluable assistance of those who have contributed to the compilation of this book. They would particularly like to thank the following:

David Bradfield for the photography; Celia Dowell for the knitting section; Freddie, Sonam and Vivie for modelling; Gwyn Lewis for typographic design; Liberty & Co. for the loan of fashion items; Leslie Spurway for typing; and those who worked so hard on the production of the book in both Britain and the USA: Ann Bond; Reg Boorer; Jackie Fortey; Lynn Franklin; Penny Hobson; Diane Huntzicker; Clive Sutherland.

Very special thanks from the author to:

Mary St. John who buys the hats; Vera Yanishek who makes them; and Charlotte Parry-Crooke who gave her invaluable enthusiastic editorial all.

Publishers' Note
All the measurements in this book are given in both imperial and metric systems. The metric measurements have been rounded up or down to the nearest half centimetre when absolutely precise equivalents are not necessary.

Library of Congress Cataloging in Publication Data
Couldridge, Alan
    The hat book.
    (A Spectrum book)
    Includes index.
    1. Hats I. Dowell, Celia, joint author.
II. Title.
TT 655. C68   646. 5'04   80-19318
ISBN 0-13-384222-3
ISBN 0-13-384214-2 (pbk.)

First published in Great Britain in 1980 by
B.T. Batsford Ltd, London

First published in the United States of America
and Canada in 1980 by Prentice-Hall Inc., Englewood Cliffs,
New Jersey 07632

Created, designed and produced by Ventura Publishing Ltd.,
44 Uxbridge Street, London W8 7TG, England

A SPECTRUM BOOK

Filmsetting by Tradespools Limited, Frome, Somerset
Colour origination by D.S. Colour International Limited, London
Printed and bound in Singapore by Tien Wah Press (Pte.) Limited

Prentice-Hall of Canada Ltd, Toronto

Contents

Introduction

Hats! Cloches, berets, turbans, caps, scarves, pull-ons, trilbies, panamas, sou'westers, straws, circlets, headdresses – all these and many, many more are just as an important part of fashion today as hats and headwear have always been in history. Though for many people nowadays a hat is not the first choice of accessory with which to round off an outfit, shoes, bag and gloves often seeming more obvious because of their functional nature, hats do still play a significant role.

Open any glossy magazine, take a look at any high street fashion store window and the chances are that you will see hats in the photographs or displayed with the merchandise. View the work of the leading clothing designers, watch the seasonal fashion shows of the top French and Italian houses, even the artwork of young students, and you will seldom find fashions shown or drawn without the total look made complete by the successful and appropriate use of millinery. For the professional this accessory is as important an element of fashion as any other item of clothing.

Just as much as other accessories and clothes, hats are indicators of fashion styles and trends. One only has to think of scarves with ties twisted round the forehead, the symbol of the ethnic styles of the mid-70s, or the nostalgic revivals in dress that regularly appear which require the correct period headwear to give credence to the style: 30s slouched Garbo felts, 40s pillboxes, and even chiffon scarves and Donovan caps from the 60s.

However, as conventions of dress have become more relaxed generally, hats have become less of a formal necessity (compared to not long ago when one simply 'was not

dressed' without the obligatory hat and gloves!). Despite the current lack of rules and regulations on wearing hats, modern millinery retains its traditional purposes: being functional and being decorative. The functional element is still prevalent in most official capacities – soldiers, school children, policemen, nurses and even chefs, all sport hats as part of their uniforms, and queens do still wear crowns! And for all of us, summer hats still keep the sun off the face, winter brims the rain out of the eyes, and woolly pull-ons keep the head and ears warm. Nowadays the decorative purpose of hats seems to have taken precedence over the functional. Hats are incredibly versatile and can really lift an outfit from the commonplace to the special, and of the masses of pretty styles available, there will be one to suit every occasion. Headdresses, which range from the most glamorous creations to the simplest coloured combs, are also popular and decorative. But in the end it is up to you whether you wear one or not – hats are now definitely a matter of personal choice.

As hats have assumed a less specific role in dress, so has the millinery industry changed. The local milliner around the corner is not often to be seen and hat shops festooned with creations spiked on angular chromium-plated stands are rather thin on the ground. Department stores, boutiques with small selections of accessories, and the occasional 'madame' shop are now the main retail sources for buying hats. The ready-to-wear mass production industry is in the hands of only a few companies, while real model milliners are becoming rarer. Within their employ the skilled milliner and the copyists (a skilful trade in its own right) tend to be of the older generation, and few young apprentices are to be seen. The truly genuine model hat, lovingly created out of basic materials by hand, requires a skill that a lifetime's apprenticeship hardly prepares one for.

It is however perfectly possible to produce extremely attractive and professional hats at home using only basic millinery equipment and normal dressmaking tools, and it can be very enjoyable. For anyone who likes using their hands, and loves the idea of wearing hats or headdresses, home production is definitely the answer, and not surprisingly it is becoming increasingly popular. This comprehensive book will introduce you to all the many possibilities for blocking, making, trimming and adapting a wide and versatile variety of headwear, as well as showing the marvellous potential hats have for complementing and completing a whole range of different fashion looks.

The patterns and trim suggestions given here range from very straightforward ideas to a few more complicated suggestions. For those who feel adventurous, turbans, felts and

straws can all be blocked from scratch; a good selection of fabric hats can be made up from the patterns shown and guidance is given on suitable fabric types. A mass of simple trimming ideas and step-by-step instructions are also shown for those who wish to give a more special and personal feel to an old hat, a new or self-blocked one.

Should you dream of owning a cupboard full of hats for every occasion, this book will not only give you the ideas, and start you off producing them, but if you fancy a change, also suggest how to alter them. Old hats can easily be refurbished, simple ones dressed up, overloaded styles made smarter and more classic; and you can always change manufacturers' originals if you feel the hats they offer are not for you. If you fancy a man's hat you will find all the encouragement you need – they do look good on women. Brides will find original ideas for headdresses, or if the idea of a traditional veil is preferred, you will see how to set about making it, and even how to utilize an heirloom.

Hats and hair do mix, and you can discover which cuts look best with which hat shapes, and how your hair and hat look will match with different fashions. Small neat hats will help generous collars and large shoulders, while long slinky bodices and lean neck lines look good beneath large brims. Men's hats are perfect for masculine style clothes like suits, trenchcoats and other sporty garments; softer brims go better with pretty dresses and silky coats. Chic turbans will set off wide shouldered crêpe jackets; keep the head small and neat, the hair lost inside, and the shoulders thus emphasized.

Wear hats at any time of night or day, during any season of the year. Should your predeliction be for disco dancing, complete a glamorous look with the gleam of a shiny head hugging skull cap, alight with sparkling diamanté on lurex, or a sequin sprinkled veiling headdress. For the most casual of daytime outfits complete with an informal cotton cloche.

For cold winter days in the country try knitted pull-ons or old flying helmets. If your country outfit is reminiscent of a man's shooting or walking suit (complete with leather patches on elbows and shoulder) what else is there to add but a tweedy trilby with trout flies in the head band or a faithful corduroy cap. For summer, try a rough woven natural straw with a large brim when basking in the sun on a far-off exotic beach, or remain cool in an open weave wheat and flower trimmed hat and a floral summer dress. Whatever type of hat you are looking for, whatever type of outfit you want to match it to, you will find most of the answers here; and remember that hats are good for confidence on all occasions!

Hats in Fashion

Hat styles are so varied that they can work well in all fashion contexts. Wear them at any time of year and any time of day. The right hat, whether practical or purely decorative, will always put the finishing touch to your outfit.

For winter wear, heavy warm coats with distinctive trimmings worn with matching or toning fur and checked wool hats.

For summer wear, a giant straw with a beachy gingham tie-on skirt, or a neat stitched cotton cloche to match an over-sized soft linen jacket.

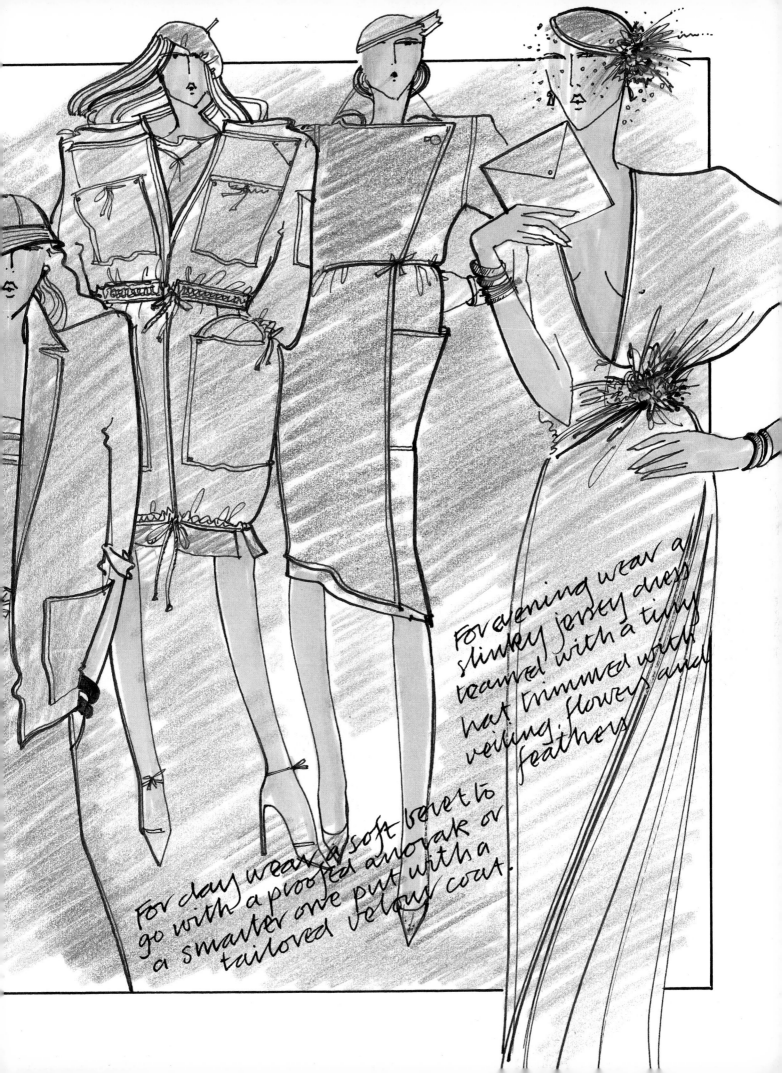

For evening wear a slinky jersey dress teamed with a tiny hat trimmed with veiling, flowers and feathers.

For day wear a soft beret to go with a proofed anorak or a smarter one put with a tailored velour coat.

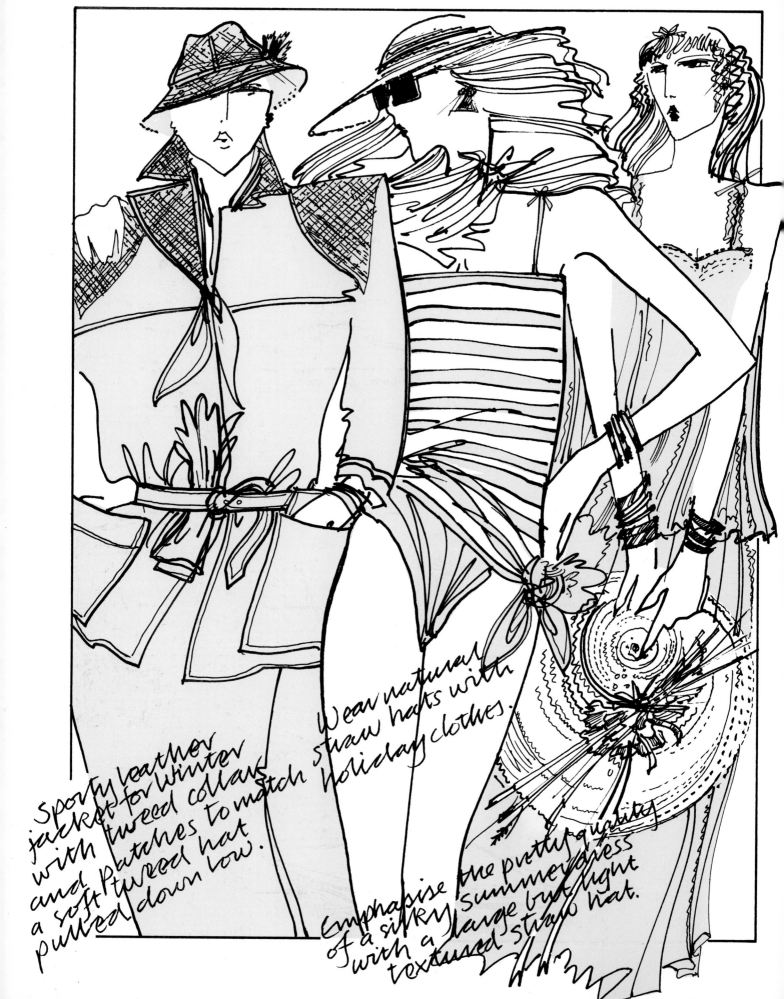

Sporty leather
jacket for winter
with tweed collars
and patches to match
a soft tweed hat
pulled down low.

Wear natural
straw hats with
holiday clothes.

Emphasise the pretty quality
of a silky summer dress
with a large but light
textured straw hat.

Basic Hat Types

However many variations on the hat can be found in fashionable modern millinery, and however many glossy photographs of different hat styles fill magazines or are displayed in department store windows, they can all be traced back to a few basic types which are shown here.

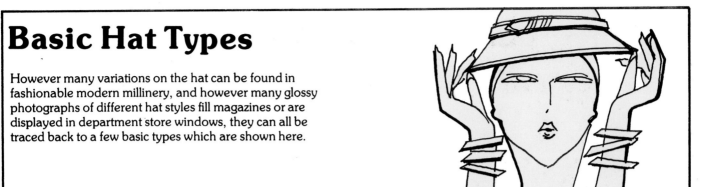

Cloche · Bonnet · Headscarf · Breton · Flying Helmet · Trilby · Pillbox · Turban · Beret · Boater · Skull Cap · Picture Hat · Cap · Fur Hat · Stetson · Knit Pull-on · Toque · Sombrero · Headdress

Millinery Terms

Although this book is designed for the non-specialist hat maker, it will be necessary during the course of describing hat styles and methods of production to use certain millinery terms, and to mention the basic foundation materials needed for the construction of hats. Those listed below with simple explanations are the most commonly used.

Terms Used in Millinery

Crown The top of the hat above the brim, the bottom part of which forms the head fitting.

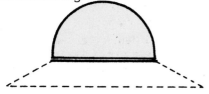

Sectional Crown Pieces of fabric (usually 5, 6 or 7 sections) machine stitched together to form the top part of the hat above the brim.

Brim The rim of the hat below the crown.

Under Brim The underside of the rim of the hat; this term is used when two layers of material make up the brim.

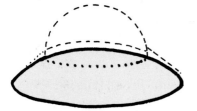

Peak The projecting part of the brim of a cap.

Tip The uppermost part of the crown when the tip and sideband method is used to construct a crown. It is usually oval in shape.

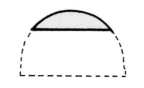

Sideband The side part of a hat's crown which runs round the crown beneath the tip. The sideband is usually joined with a seam at the centre back.

Head Fitting The line inside the crown that touches the head. A grosgrain band is usually inserted round the head fitting for comfort and as a subtle size adjustment.

Head Ribbon A grosgrain band, curved and cut to size, which is sewn within the crown to form the head fitting.

Head Band Any ribbon or other trim which is added to the hat round the outside of the head fitting line.

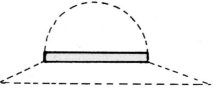

Trimming Any decorative feature which is added to the basic hat.

Grain The weave of fabric seen in the threads running the length and width of the fabric.

Bias The true diagonal of the fabric. One of the golden rules of millinery is always to use the fabric on the bias or cross.

Crossway The cross of a fabric is the same as the bias. The true cross or bias is found by placing one selvedge of the fabric to the other. The long edge of the triangle thus formed is the fabric's true cross.

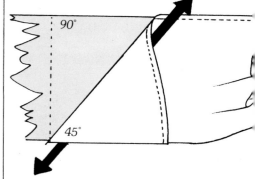

Lay A term used to describe the placing and arrangement of the pieces of a pattern on the fabric.

Blocks

Blocking The shaping of fabric by dampening or steaming it.

Blocks The wooden forms on which foundation fabrics and fabrics themselves are shaped. They come in all shapes and sizes and can be made to order by skilled blockmakers, though basic blocks may be bought off the shelf. Wooden blocks form the basis of model and home millinery, while metal blocks fitted to a hydraulic press are used in mass production.

Crown Block The crown block is the most useful and common block. It is oval with a rounded top like the shape of a head.

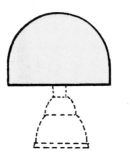

Skull Block This block is shaped very like the head itself with the back cut away as though into the neck.

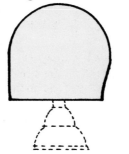

Brim Blocks The shapes on which brims are blocked are infinitely variable but the most common and useful is a medium sized block with a 20cm (8in) diameter and a 22° brim angle. Both brim and crown blocks should ideally be 1.3cm(½in) larger than your head size.

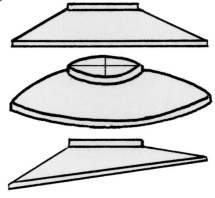

Dolly A mock-up of the head made in linen which will take pins easily and should be in your own size.

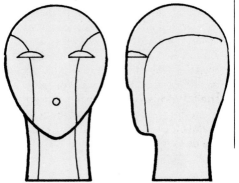

Stand A turned wooden support on which blocks are stood while being worked on.

Hoods

Hoods This is the collective name given to straws or felts pre-manufactured into approximate hat shapes. Two basic types are commonly used: the cone and the capeline.

Cone The cone hood is suitable for blocking into small brimmed or brimless hats.

Capeline The capeline hood comes with a small crown and flat brim and is suitable for blocking into larger brimmed styles.

Felts The name given to pre-formed hoods made out of fur or wool felt, one of the basic hat materials. Felt hoods are available in many finishes and colours.

Straws The name given to hoods made out of straw, another basic hat material. Like felts, they come in many finishes and colours.

Foundation Fabrics

Foundation Fabrics Fabrics out of which the basic hat shapes are constructed. These shapes will then be covered with the chosen hat fabric.

Spartre/Espartre Woven straw sheets covered in muslin which when dampened can be blocked or shaped, and which retain their blocked shape when dry.

Blocking Net Open net which has a resinous feel and is available in a wide range of colours. It can be shaped or blocked when steamed and will retain its shape when dry.

Leno A fine net which is used for making good overlapped spartre joins.

Tarlatan Another type of fine net which is most useful as a mounting fabric, and which can be used for pattern making.

Construction Materials

Millinery Wire Wire covered in fine cotton thread. It is used for firming up brim edges and comes in varying weights. Use the lightest wire that will do the job satisfactorily.

Stiffeners Stiffeners are types of varnish used to give body to fabric, felt and straw. Several different types are manufactured for different purposes.

Linings Linings are used inside hat crowns if the insides are untidy. If they are neat, it is not necessary to line them. Crown linings can be purchased ready-made in tip and sideband form.

Grosgrain Ribbon A corded ribbon which is the most common of all hat trimming ribbons. It is also used for head fitting ribbons and is good for binding brim edges. It curves easily as it has no finished edge and it can therefore be put round curved surfaces after stretching one edge under the iron. It is available in many sizes, and these are usually referred to by numbers; for example a 1.3cm (½in) ribbon is No 3 and a 2.5cm (1in) ribbon is No 5.

The Millinery Trade

Model Hat A hand-made hat. This term is used to describe a unique hat but may now more commonly describe a short run of a particular hat.

Mass Production Hat A factory-made product with a minimum of hand work.

Milliner A skilled craftsman who is capable of creating by hand a hat from beginning to end.

Copyist The person who reproduces a number of facsimiles from an original sample.

Tools and Equipment for Making Hats

Many of the hats in this book can be made or trimmed without the use of specialist millinery equipment, and if you are interested in sewing, you will probably already own most of the items listed under general equipment. However you will also need a few basic millinery tools and blocks (also listed below), but these can be kept to a minimum.

General Equipment

Electric sewing machine A hand machine can be used but much millinery work requires two hands to control the work.

Iron An iron with a chromium plated bottom is best, since an aluminum bottomed one will mark certain materials, such as white straw.

Scissors Several pairs for different jobs will be needed: large cutting out shears with 20.3cm(8in) or 22.9cm(9in) blades; small sharp scissors with 10.2cm(4in) or 12.7cm(5in) blades; and a pair of paper scissors for cutting paper, spartre and straw.

Ironing board

Tape measure

Dressmaker's steel pins Use 2.9cm(1 ³⁄₁₆in) long pins for best results.

Thimble This is essential for millinery work, since much of it is quite tough and it can be painful to work without one.

Tea kettle Use an old-fashioned kettle rather than an electric model with a cut-out mechanism. It will enable you to steam hats for as long as you need.

Pliers A long nosed pair with a wire cutting edge is best.

Drawing or 'T' pins Avoid small bulletin board pins which bend and break easily; good quality drawing pins are much stronger and easier to use.

Specialist Equipment

Tailor pressing cushion or ham This will be very useful when working with rounded surfaces.

Spiral This sprung metal ring is used to hold fabrics, straws and felts in place on crown blocks.

Blocks You will need a wooden crown block and one brim block to begin with, both in your own size if you are making hats for yourself.

Stand This will hold your block while you are working on it.

Dolly A linen dolly head will be needed to work on, but it will also be useful for assessing shapes.

Needles A range of longer needles is required for the curved work that forms the bulk of millinery sewing. The needles you will need are called 'Straws', sizes 6, 7 and 8.

Pressing pad This can be made by folding a piece of cotton fabric over several times and machining it all over to compress it into a pad of about 10cm(4in) square. It will be particularly useful when ironing against your hand.

Brushes Several cheap 2.5cm(1in) paint brushes will be needed for use with different types of stiffener.

Fabrics for Use in Millinery

The variety of fabrics that can be used for making hats is so vast that it is only possible to give a general guide to their choice here. However, in the following chapters more specific information is given on the suitability of different fabrics for different hat types.

Since you will be working on the round surface when making hats, the most important factor to consider when choosing a fabric is whether it will block well. This is to say, can the fabric be stretched over a curved surface, steamed and pinned, and when it is dry, will it retain its blocked shape. Two other points to think about are whether the fabric is light enough to make a comfortable hat, and whether it will make up cleanly.

As a general rule, man-made fabrics tend not to block well (though they may be used for hats that require no blocking), while most natural fabrics, apart from the heavier tweeds, have all the properties necessary to make them suitable for hat making. Among the many natural fabrics that work well in millinery are cottons (such as gingham, madras, seersucker, denim, sailcloth, gabardine, chintz, corduroy and velvet), wools (such as light tweeds, flannel, gabardine, crêpe and velour) and silks (such as Thai, Indian and oriental silks, twill, tweed and raw silk, foulard, crêpe, brocade, velvet and satin).

Linens will also work well in millinery, and furnishing weights with their attractive textures make especially interesting fashion fabrics. Pile fabrics (such as velvets and fur piles) make up well though they require careful handling. Lace will block reasonably but not over excessive curves, though motifs can be cut out and appliquéd separately. Leathers, suedes and furs all make excellent hats since when wet the skins will pull well and then retain their pulled shapes.

Practically none of the synthetic group of man-made fabrics are suitable for hat making. Nylons, polyesters, rayons and acetates will all resist blocking. However, blocking does become possible when man-made fibres are mixed in reasonable proportions with natural ones (as happens in so many dress weight fabrics now), and these fabrics then become suitable for use in millinery.

Most fibre mixtures and natural fibres are available in the knitted form of 'jersey'. All types of jersey are splendid for hats, since its natural stretching property makes it excellent both for draping and pulling over the round shape.

Basic Millinery Skills

Many of the hats in this book, such as those in Chapter One, can be made or trimmed by using basic dressmaking techniques. Others, such as felts and straws, will require the use of basic blocking methods, and these are described in detail in Chapters Three, Four and Five. However there are two principles that are essential in millinery, whether you are making a new hat from scratch or altering an existing one: correct sizing and correct stitching. The basic rules governing these two important aspects of millinery are explained below, eliminating the need to refer to them repeatedly when the assembling and trimming of different types of hat is described later on.

Sizing

When buying blocks or making patterns you will need to know your head size, presuming you wish to make hats for yourself. Your basic wooden blocks (crown, skull or brim) should be 1.3cm(½in) larger than your own head measurement while your canvas dolly should be the same size as your head. Should you be well over or under the average head size of 57.2cm(22½in), by 2.5cm(1in) or more, or you wish to make hats for other people, you will need to have alternative sets of blocks. Sizes can be adjusted to a certain extent in the process of making the hat but over 2.5cm (1in) would be an unreasonable amount to shrink or stretch a hat.

To measure your head, the tape should be placed around the headline, where the hat fitting would touch your head (fig 1). Make sure the tape is comfortably positioned and not too tight. This is the most basic head measurement, though for custom-made millinery others will also be taken.
Measurements over the top of the head from side to side (fig 2) and from back to front (fig 3) will also be taken in order to

check for extra wide or long heads, both of which will throw tailored brims out of line. There is no need to concern yourself with this problem unless you have noticed that brims buckle on your head. Should this be the case, make sure you obtain your blocks with the extra necessary width or length.

It is also important to get the sizing right when making soft fabric hat patterns. With this type of hat your head size will be taken into account when drafting the pattern. In calculating the sizing for a crown pattern, the sum of the component parts of the crown should add up to your head fitting measurement (fig 4). Alternatively the number of sections in the crown can be divided into your head fitting and the resulting measurement distributed equally among the sections or in some other chosen proportion (fig 5).

To calculate head fittings for brim patterns would require a complicated piece of mathematics. An easier and just as reliable way is to prepare a head wire to your own fitting (which can be retained for further use). This can be made from millinery wire, cut 7.5cm(3in) or 10.2cm(4in) larger than your head fitting, to give an overlap which is joined by wrapping thread tightly round the overlapped wire, thus forming a ring (fig 6). The ring is then bent into an oval which should feel comfortable when placed around the head line. This head wire will enable you to cut your brim patterns to the correct size (fig 7).

Stitching

There are no special millinery stitches; in fact the golden rule is to stitch as little as possible. Most stitches used in millinery are the same as those used in dressmaking but slight variations are needed in handling because of the necessity to stitch around or within curved surfaces. For this reason the long straw needles (*see* page 16) should be used. The most commonly used stitches in millinery are:

Stab Stitch (fig 8). This is a stitch which keeps the long part of the thread on the wrong side of the fabric. By putting the needle back almost exactly where it came out (on the right side of the fabric) and stabbing completely through from one side to the other, no stitch is seen on the fabric's right side.

Slip Stitch (fig 9). To hold a folded fabric to a flat one, the thread is passed along the inside of the fold and the needle picks up a small stitch on the flat fabric where it comes out, below the fold and marginally inside the line of the fold. It then passes back into the fold and repeats the action. As the stitch tightens, no thread can be seen. This stitch is particularly useful for brim edges, inserting linings, and joining crowns to brims where no head band is to be used.

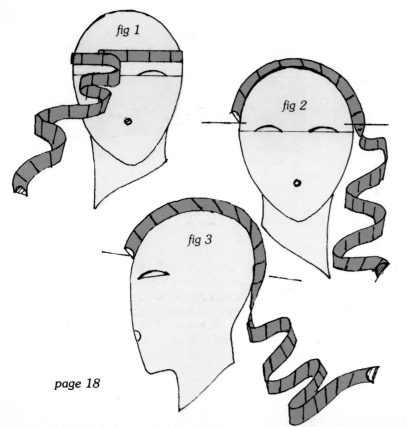

fig 1

fig 2

fig 3

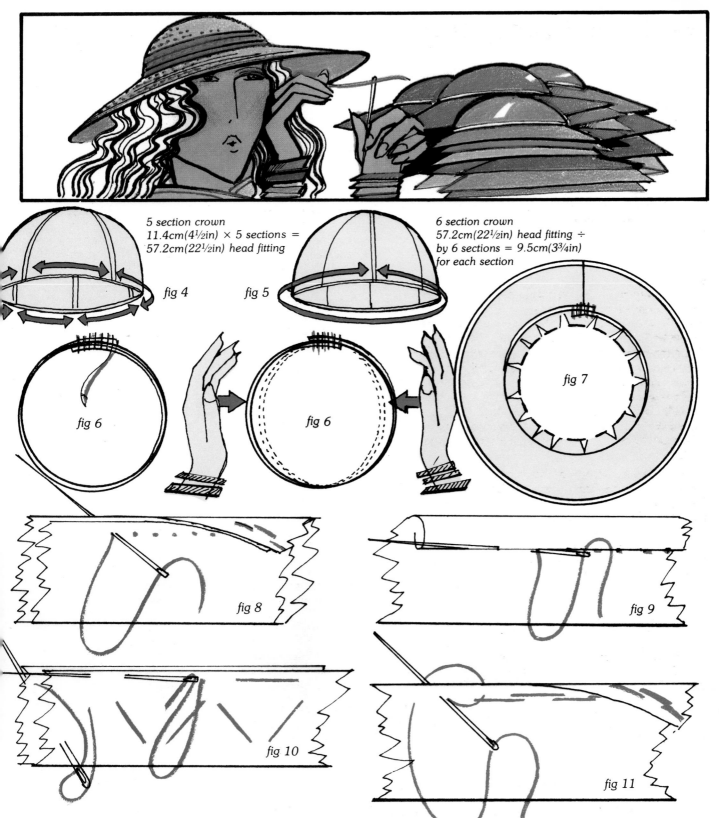

5 section crown
11.4cm(4½in) × 5 sections =
57.2cm(22½in) head fitting

fig 4   fig 5

6 section crown
57.2cm(22½in) head fitting ÷
by 6 sections = 9.5cm(3¾in)
for each section

fig 7

fig 6   fig 6

fig 8   fig 9

fig 10   fig 11

Tacking Stitch (fig 10). This large stitch is used to hold fabrics together prior to a more permanent stitch (or machining) being used. The needle is passed in and out of the fabric in large stitches in either a straight line or a zig-zag pattern. Use it on soft hats before top stitching or for holding the sections of a soft crown together temporarily while you check its appearance before machining.

Back Stitch (fig 11). In this stitch the needle is passed in and out of the fabric, travelling back a quarter of its last length each time, instead of making consistent forward progress. It is not an invisible stitch but it is a good one for joining brims and crowns together when the line of stitching is to be covered with a head band or other trimming.

Hair and Hats

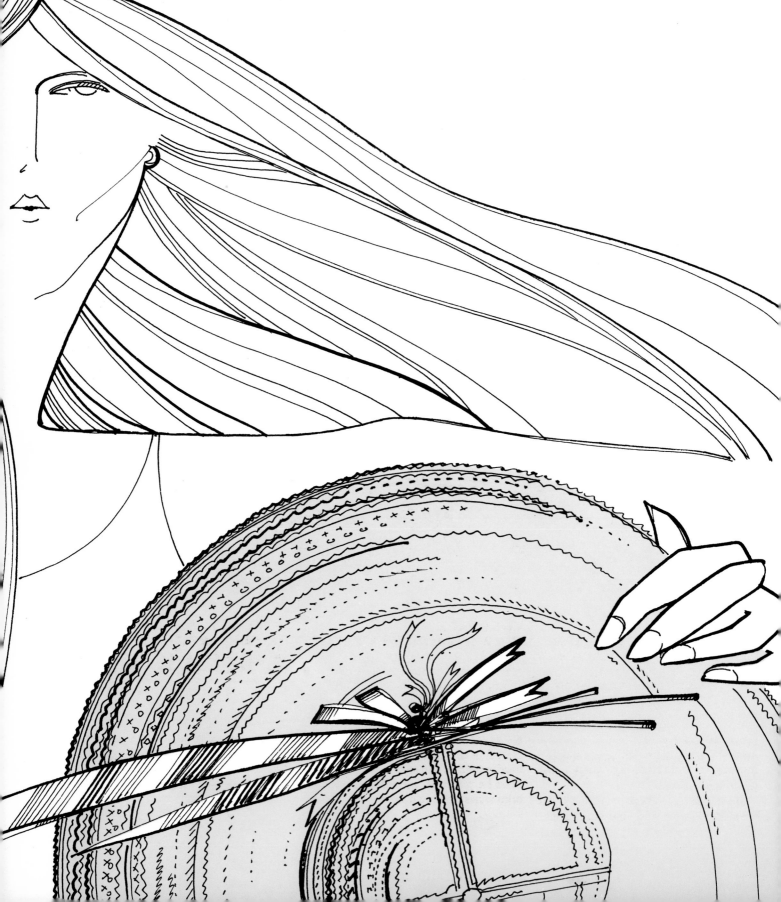

Contrary to popular belief, hair and hats do go together. Both today's fashions and the more informal life styles adopted by women require natural hair styles. Soft easily maintained hair, well shaped and skilfully cut, suits the relaxed style of dress to be found in all fashion, from jeans to evening wear. Permanent waves are now used to create easy styles and not the overstyled 'not a hair out of place' appearance that used to be the fashion. Nowadays, with every hair-cut a hat is possible.

Hair that relies for its effect on its cut alone, and not on being teased, backcombed or stuck into shape, will not be ruined by the wearing of a hat. Put on a hat. Take it off. Shake your head. Your well cut hair will fall back into place. Wear large hats, small ones, hats with veils, hats for sports, formal or evening wear. If the hair suits your face, and the hat suits your clothes, your fashion story will be complete.

The principles of which type of hair-cut suits which type of face shape are already well documented and advice abounds for the long faced, the wide faced, the long nosed, the wide eyed and so on. All have been analysed and their antidotes prescribed. Hats, however, add another dimension to this theme; listed below are some basic principles to help you choose appropriate hat types for your particular face shape and hair-cut.

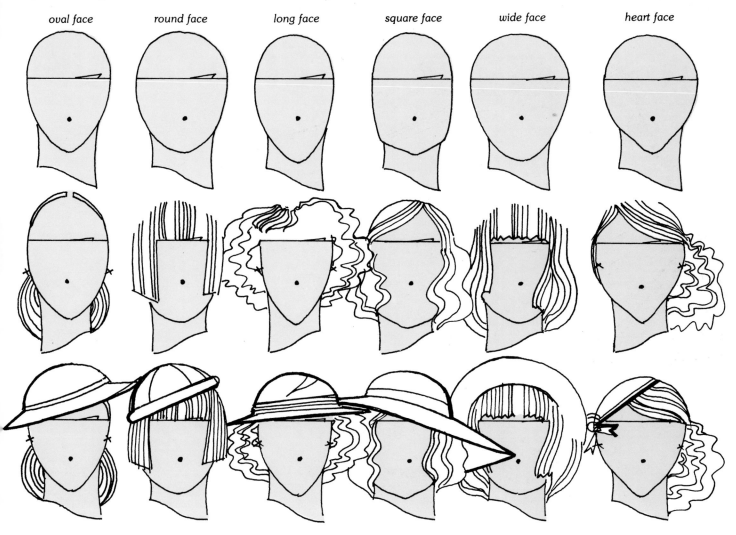

oval face   *round face*   *long face*   *square face*   *wide face*   *heart face*

OVAL FACE
Hair Swept back styles, either slick or full. Interest at back, high on head or back of neck.
Hats Streamlined shapes, worn forward. Brims turned up at back or swept up at sides.

ROUND FACE
Hair Centre partings. Sharp cut styles which break cheek lines. If longer, worn in front of ears.
Hats Medium or small brims, neat styles worn stylishly forward, or on the slant.

LONG FACE
Hair Wide looks with high fullness, in soft styles.
Hats Medium to wide brims, worn straight or forward. Straight, sharp styles.

SQUARE FACE
Hair Full and soft. Low cheek interest in hard-edged or soft styles.
Hats Large brims with soft lines. Open brim styles framing hair.

WIDE FACE
Hair Fringes with middle neck fullness.
Hats Off the face styles, bretons or back worn pillboxes. Sombrero shapes worn high.

HEART FACE
Hair Side partings, side swept styles.
Hats Side worn brims, small one-sided hats or hair decorations.

Hair and Hats

Purposeful square-cut hair style looks splendid with soft felt beret worn well over to one side.

Exuberant frizzier hair style is the perfect vehicle for a hair decoration like this flower and ribbon example.

Longer hair bunched at the back of the neck sets off a tidy knitted pull-on hat nicely.

Neat hats need neat hair. Swept-back style, kept close to the head, and pulled into a roll or bun, looks right with a tiny hat and decorative veil.

Brimmed Panama straw hat adds to the youthful feel of a long, straight hair-cut with a full fringe.

More generous, billowy hair effect is complemented by a giant brimmed hat with large areas of the underbrim visible.

Fabric Hats from Flat Patterns

For the home hat maker, soft hats with unstructured shapes are the most straightforward to make. The range of this type of hat – from jersey pull-ons to wintery trapper hats, summer cloches to stitched berets – is particularly wide. Despite this variety of possible styles, they all share one basic feature: all are developed from flat paper patterns, and since their construction is more like dressmaking than real millinery, they are often referred to as 'dressmaker hats'. Unlike blocked fabric hats (laid on spartre or net foundations), no base is required other than a flat cut interfacing to give body to the flimsy fabrics they are sometimes made of.

The most common and versatile soft hat shape made from a flat pattern is the stitched cloche, so named on account of its brim shape, which is often machine stitched all over to give body and decoration. This infinitely adaptable hat can be made up in all kinds of fabric, and trimmed in a mass of original ways. Pattern, fabric, size and trim can all be used to give different results – variations of this classic style are really endless.

Most soft hats can be constructed from any fabric of dress to light coat weight, though practically any material can be used, even relatively unsympathetic ones, or particularly thick fabrics. Notes on the suitability of different fabric types are given on page 26.

To make soft hats you will require only basic dressmaking equipment. The scaled-down patterns on the following pages give step-by-step instructions for cutting out and assembling the hats, and these can be modified according to taste. Brim angles and sizes can be varied, and height, shape and crown pattern segments can be adapted to suit any mood or occasion, from smart daywear to casual country or even decorative evening looks.

No serious blocking is necessary when making fabric hats but if you have invested in a crown block or a dolly, it will be useful for setting crowns, though this can easily be done on your own head. Warmth and natural dampness will set the fabric and flatten the seams – the resulting neatness will give your hat a really professional finish.

Fabric Favourites

Soft hats from flat patterns can be made in a mass of different attractive fabrics. In fact you can use almost any material as long as it is not too heavy (coat weight) or too stiff. All kinds of cotton are ideal, and cords, canvas and even leathers work well too. Wools and tweeds are very suitable but not those with loose open weaves as the interlinings will show through.

Each fabric will create its own individual look even if you have used the same basic hat shape. For a traditional sporty feel try rustic country tweeds – silk or velvet for a more sophisticated image. Personalize with inventive trims and the possibilities are endless. Although the hats shown here are mostly of the cloche type with stitched brim, all the suggested fabrics are suitable for any type of soft sewn hat including those described in the patterns on the following pages.

1 Muslin, the basic raw cotton fabric used for toiles in dressmaking, makes up neatly, but use the tailoring weight since it gives a better finish.

2 Woollen suiting, Prince of Wales check, and fine herringbone weave all look good in this style. Worsted, gabardine and flannel also tailor well and can look very smart.

3 Harris tweed, like other rough tweeds, makes an excellent sporting version of the soft sewn hat.

4 Raw silk has a really expensive texture. Thai silk and silk with tweed or twill finishes give a rich, exotic look to the classic cloche. Only the very finest silks should be avoided since they require a lot of interlining which will spoil their natural quality.

5 Vinyl or vinyl coated fabrics can be used to make rainhats in the cloche style, but remember to top stitch the seams open as vinyl will not block. Try an oilcloth sou'wester; it is only a cloche with a long back to the brim.

6 Gingham is the youngest and most summery of cottons. Different sized checks in the crown sections and contrasting colour combinations can both be used effectively.

7 Seersucker has an attractive puckered line throughout which gives a light summery texture, which can be enhanced if the fabric is stitched all over.

8 Basic tailoring construction fabrics, duck and canvas make up crisply and come in natural creams or khaki. Try using hessian or collar canvas – even scrim.

9 Both Liberty print Varuna wool (the challis wool made famous by Liberty's and available in their traditional prints) and Jubilee, their challis blend mixture, make up very well. Try teaming plain and printed together.

10 Satin can look marvellous in the evening, but take care to keep the brim neat when making up. Lurex thread stitching will add a touch of glitter and a veil will overdo it beautifully.

11 White cotton drill is sporty and definitely for high summer. Sailors wear it, and so do cricketers, who have adopted it instead of their traditional cap.

12 Liberty print Tana Lawn is cool and classic. The old patterns are still the most charming, though sadly rather out of fashion at the moment.

13 Terrycloth makes up well. Use it with other cottons to give stiffness or interline it. Perfect for covering wet hair. Try velvety velour for a more sophisticated look.

14 Light furnishing fabrics, especially cottons, look good and are quite unusual.

15 Chintz is glossy when plain and elegant when printed with floral patterns.

16 Velvet is a traditional millinery fabric but watch the pile and do not over handle it. Panne velvet is silky and charmingly old-fashioned.

17 Wear it and wash it denim. The older and more faded it becomes, the more it will be admired. If it starts to fray, treasure it!

18 Corduroy makes a very comfortable hat. It is available in fine needle cord to heavy jumbo. Be careful with the direction when cutting and do not top stitch too close together so as not to destroy the pile lines.

19 Lace will look very pretty, but put in a self-coloured blocking net interlining to give it body. Try to match up the lace pattern on the top and bottom brims.

20 All jerseys are excellent for soft hats. Silky jerseys are quite exotic, while angora jersey's fluffy effect is luxurious and feather light, but warm for winter wear.

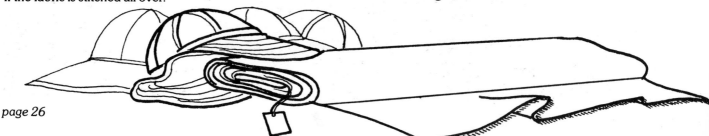

Simple Soft Cloche

The simple stitched cloche with a six section crown is one of the most popular hat shapes. It is easy to make from the flat pattern given here, and is very versatile. Try it in any one of a wide variety of suitable fabrics (*see* page 26 for lots of suggestions), adapt it to your own requirements and personalize it with a mass of different trims.

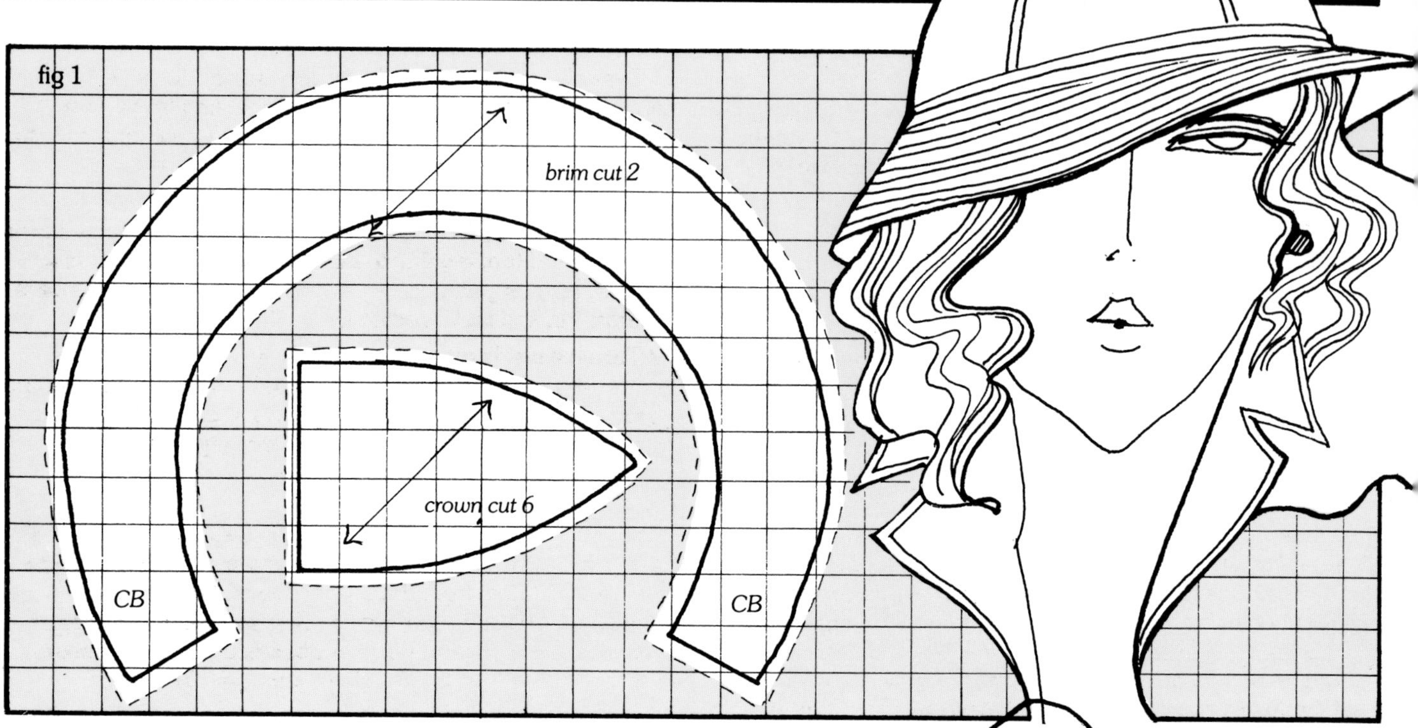

fig 1

brim cut 2

crown cut 6

CB

CB

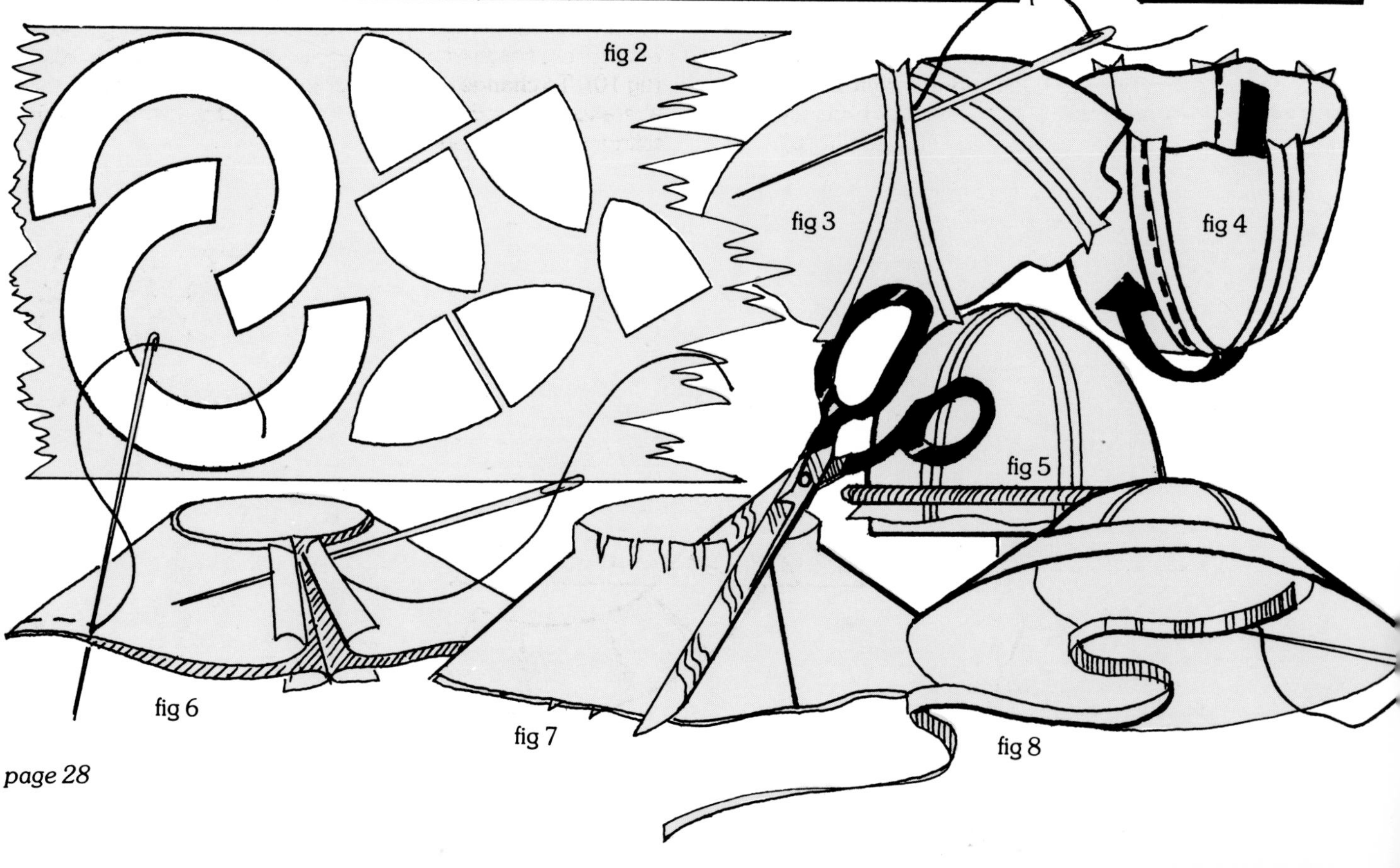

fig 2

fig 3

fig 4

fig 5

fig 6

fig 7

fig 8

Materials

½m(½yd) chosen fabric
½m(½yd) interfacing (type depending on the fabric weight)
If chosen fabric is firm, it is not necessary to line crown
Grosgrain ribbon for head fitting

Method

1 The pattern given is ¼ scale for a 57.2cm(22½in) head fitting (fig 1). Scale up on to graph paper all measurements except seam allowances ×4. For other head sizes see page 18.

2 Place scaled-up pattern on fabric following suggested lay (fig 2) and cut out fabric and interfacing on the cross. For interfacing, cut seam allowances for head fitting only. Mount fabric on to interfacing by zig-zag tacking all over.

3 To make up the crown, tack three of the six crown sections together (fig 3), machine stitch and press open seams. Top stitch seams open. Repeat process with other three sections and join two halves together with one final seam right over the top (fig 4). Top stitch this final seam open, working around the inside of the now formed crown. Block the crown by steaming over a crown block, using a spiral or 'T' pins to keep it in place (fig 5).

4 To make up the brim, first join back seams of both top and bottom brims, and press open. Place brims right side to right side, line up centre back seams, and then tack brim edges together. Machine stitch, turn through and press (fig 6).

5 Tack all over brim to make it easier to control while handling. Top stitch round the brim, working from outer edge inward; leave machine foot's width (or half foot's width if you prefer) between rows of stitching.

6 To join crown to brim, first clip seam allowances round brim fitting 2cm(¾in) apart (fig 7). Turn crown edge under or if head band trim is going to be added, cut off and use raw edge. Place clipped brim under crown, matching centre back seams. Pin and tack in position.

7 Turn hat inside out and machine stitch brim and crown together from the inside. Insert curved 1.3cm(½in) grosgrain head ribbon around head fitting with same line of machine stitching, or slip it in by hand afterwards (fig 8).

Pattern Adaptations

You can alter this basic pattern for a soft stitched cloche in a number of ways. To increase or decrease the size of the brim add to or subtract from the outer edge of the brim only. Adjust the pattern in proportion, always leaving the front of the brim longer than the back for balance; the sides can be adjusted according to the style required (fig 9).

To increase the angle of the brim, slash brim pattern evenly to make overlapping darts. Do not try to increase angle by taking from back seam only as this will produce a cone shape (fig 10). To change the shape of the crown, make any alterations towards the top of the crown otherwise the head fitting will be affected (fig 11).

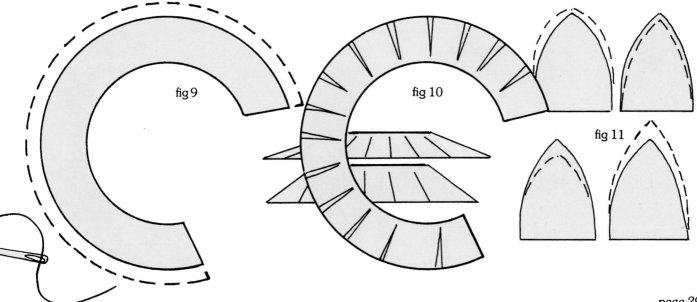

fig 9

fig 10

fig 11

Fatigue Cap with Earflaps

This smart but comfortable military cap with earflaps can be made out of a variety of different fabric weights. In crisp cotton with the earflaps turned up it will be cool for summer; quilt it and turn up your coat collar and you'll be protected against even the coldest day.

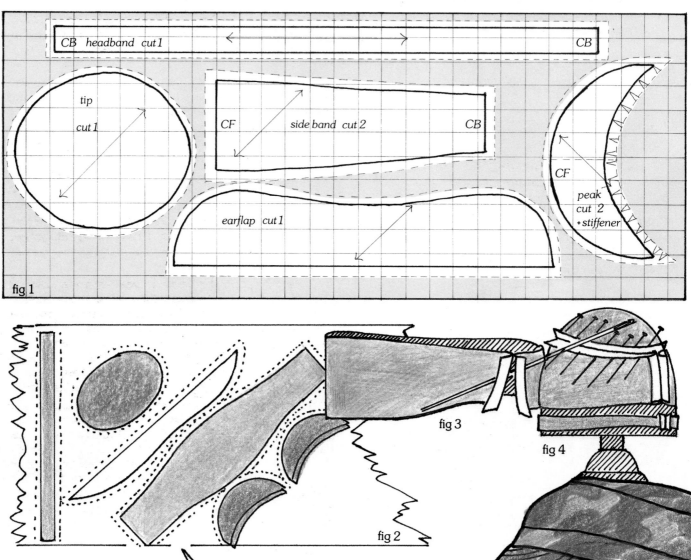

CB   headband cut 1   CB

tip
cut 1

CF   side band cut 2   CB

CF

peak
cut 2
+ stiffener

earflap cut 1

fig 1

fig 3

fig 4

fig 2

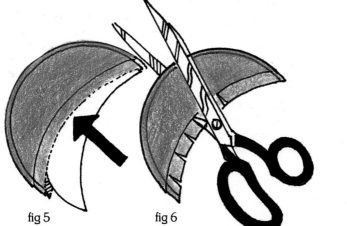

fig 5   fig 6

Materials

½m(½yd) stiff cotton, denim or canvas
½m(½yd) tailoring weight interfacing
Small piece of cotton or soft wool for earflap lining
Buckram or cardboard for peak stiffener
Grosgrain ribbon for head fitting

Method

1 The pattern given is a ¼ scale for a 57.2m(22½in) head fitting (fig 1). Scale up on to graph paper all measurements except seam allowances ×4. For other head sizes see page 18. Remember to mark on your pattern: centre back on tip; centre front on peak and head band.

2 Place scaled-up pattern on fabric following suggested lay (fig 2) and cut out fabric and interfacings on the cross. Cut out soft earflap lining and peak stiffener. All linings, except earflap lining, can be cut without seam allowances. Mount fabric on to interfacing by zig-zag tacking all over.

3 To construct the earflap, stitch earflap and corresponding lining together right side to right side around the outer edge. Turn through, press and top stitch. Treat as one fabric from now on.

4 To make the crown, tack two sideband pieces together at centre front and centre back to form a circle (fig 3). Machine, press seams open and top stitch.

5 Pin, and then tack, tip into made-up sideband on your crown block, placing the right side to the wood (fig 4). Set tip in evenly, to avoid catching any folds in the seam when machining. Machine stitch tip and sideband together. Press seams open on the block, and then top stitch from inside the now formed crown.

6 Tack, and then machine stitch, head band at centre back. Pin, and then tack, head band to the crown, matching centre back seams. Machine stitch. Fold head band under along the head fitting line and tack up.

7 To make the peak, place the two peak sections together, right side to right side. Tack, and then machine stitch them together around the outer edge only. Turn through, and then press. Insert peak stiffener between two layers of peak (fig 5). Machine stitch all over peak from outer edge to seam allowance at regular intervals of a machine foot's width (or half a machine foot's width if you prefer). Clip seam allowances 2cm(¾in) apart around peak head fitting (fig 6).

8 To join crown, earflaps and peak, place clipped peak under set-in head band, matching centre front to centre front. Pin, and then tack, peak to crown. Place earflap under set-in head band, to overlap peak on inside by 2.5cm(1in) on either side. Pin, and then tack, earflap to crown. Machine stitch peak and earflap to the head band with one line of stitching. Insert curved 1.3cm(½in) grosgrain head ribbon around the head fitting with the same line of machine stitching, or slip it in by hand afterward.

Pattern Adaptations

This basic pattern for a fatigue cap with earflaps can be adapted in several ways according to taste. To increase or decrease the size of the peak, add or subtract evenly from the outer edge of the peak only (fig 7). To increase or decrease the angle of the peak, alter the head fitting curve. The more the head fitting line is curved, the steeper the peak will be; the flatter the head fitting curve, the straighter the peak (fig 8). To alter the height of the crown, add to either the sideband or the head band, but do not adjust the length as the head fitting will be affected (fig 9).

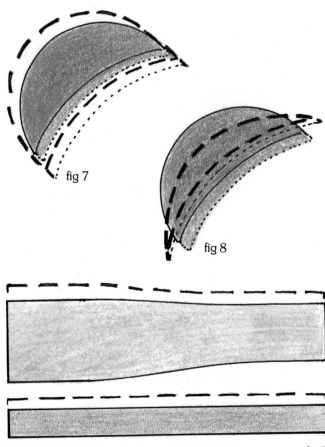

fig 7

fig 8

fig 9

Soft Stitched Beret

An attractive soft stitched beret can be just as adaptable as
other types of fabric hats made from flat patterns. It can be
made out of many fabric types but softer ones are particularly
suitable. Adjust the pattern to vary its shape and effect, giving
it more fullness or a smaller, neater feel. Create a wide range
of looks with this stylish hat – from crisp and tailored by day,
to subtle and glossy by night.

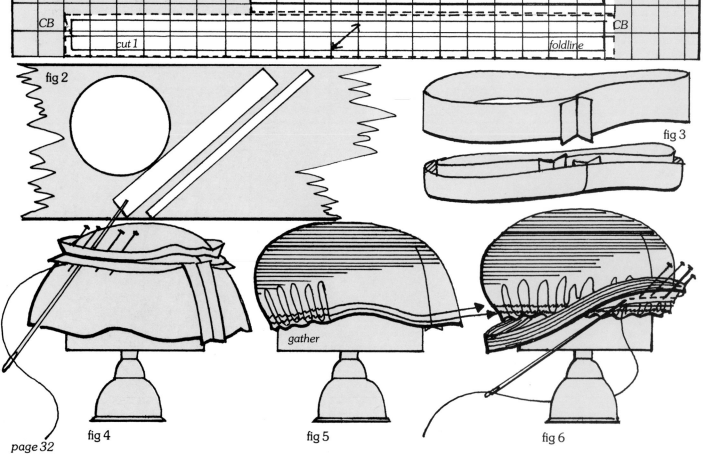

fig 1

cut 1

CF   CB

cut 1

cut to fold   CB

gather

CB   cut 1   CB

foldline

fig 2

fig 3

gather

fig 4   fig 5   fig 6

Materials
½m(½yd) chosen fabric
½m(½yd) interfacing.
Grosgrain ribbon for head fitting

Method

1 The pattern given is ¼ scale for a 57.2cm(22½in) head fitting (fig 1). Scale up on to graph paper all measurements except seam allowances ×4. For other head sizes see page 18.

2 Place scaled-up pattern on fabric following suggested lay (fig 2) and cut out fabric and interfacing. Interfacings should be cut without seam allowances. Mount fabric on to interfacing by zig-zag tacking all over.

3 To make up the head band, join the centre back seam. Press seam open. Stitch all round head band at regular intervals of half a machine foot's width. Fold over wrong side to wrong side to form head band and gently press (fig 3).

4 To make the crown, tack and then machine the sideband at the centre back to form a circle. Press open seam and then top stitch. Stitch all round sideband at regular intervals of half a machine foot's width. Stitch round tip in a similar fashion.

5 Pin, and then tack, tip into sideband (fig 4). A crown block will help control this operation but the pattern is not supposed to fit the crown block. Set tip into sideband evenly, so that no folds or tucks are machined in. Machine stitch together, and press seam open against the block. Top stitch seam from inside the now formed crown.

6 To join the crown to the head band, ease sideband into head band. Gather sideband to the head fitting size, using two lines of largest machine stitching for best results (fig 5).

7 Join gathered crown to the outer half of the folded head band, right side to right side (fig 6). Machine stitch, turn out and press. Hem raw edge of folded head band to the inside of hat. Slip in a 1.3cm(½in) grosgrain head fitting ribbon to neaten the hemline.

Pattern Adaptations

The shape of this soft stitched beret can be altered in several different ways. To increase or decrease the overall size of the beret, add to or subtract equally from the tip and the ends of the sideband, remembering that the sideband measurement must equal the circumference of the tip (fig 7). To alter the height of the beret, add to or subtract from the top edge of the sideband (fig 8). To give the beret a more rounded look, dart the tip but add to its circumference to compensate for the smaller tip. Top stitch between the darts in different patterns (fig 9).

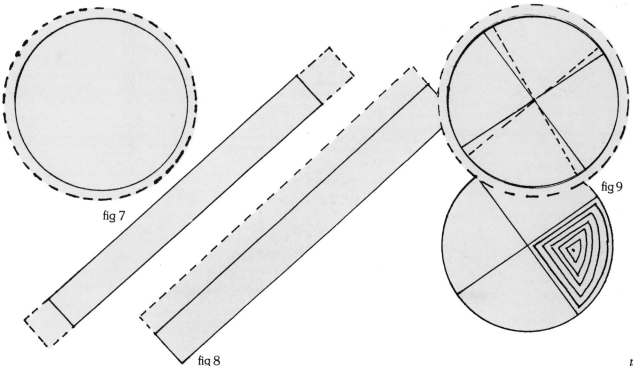

fig 7

fig 8

fig 9

Fashion Looks

Even the simplest cloche can become an integrated part of your fashion look if made in the same fabric as a part of your outfit. Because it can be made in so many different types of fabric, you can match it to any look – from winter tweeds to summer cottons.

Team a soft wool fabric hat with a matching shawl and co-ordinating gathered skirt for cooler days.

Look good on deck in a traditionally styled blazer and cotton cloche in a similarly strong colour.

or hotter summer days link the colours of a patterned fabric hat and a cool simple cotton print sundress.

swimsuit and matching stitched terry towelling sun hat to make a summer splash.

Try a stitched cloche sun hat with a halter-necked T-shirt in the same colour and hip-tied sarong.

More Fabric Hat Styles

A fur fabric pull-on hat (set on to a fabric crown), could be made out of leather or suede, or even an all-fur fabric, if you like the idea of a giant Cossack hat. Make the crown as if for a simple cloche (page 29). The fur 'roll' is only a folded head band which is set into the crown like a brim, and then turned up from the outer edge. The deep pile of the fur will give the rounded look, but wadding may be added inside the roll to give it a more padded effect.

To make a cotton baseball cap, you can use the system outlined on page 30 for the Fatigue Cap with Earflaps. Alternatively you can make the cap with a six section crown (with eyelets), as shown here. Add an elasticated strap and buckle for an adjustable head fitting, and don't forget to stick your pony tail through the back, if you want to look like a bobby soxer!

This soft jersey pull-on hat looks splendid in glittery jersey or even with adhesive diamanté studs added. It can be hand knitted or made up in fluffy or silky jersey. Simply make a double tube with neatened seams and a set-in tip marginally tighter than your crown block or dolly. Pull the tube over the crown block and tightly roll up tube from bottom. The back seam will be neat on the roll since it is a double tube. Then slip stitch the roll around the hat. Good accurate machine stitching and hand sewing are necessary to make this fabric hat look really good.

A trapper's hat will look good in sheepskin or Canadian checked wool or even in fashionable quilted cotton and man-made pile fabric. Whichever you choose, make sure the seam allowances turn to the right side so that the fur or pile will show up in coloured lines. You will need to block the four section crown to shape it. If you use sheepskin, it will, like leather, block marvellously by wetting it (after it is sewn together), pulling it tightly over the crown block and then leaving till dry.

Scarves as Hats

The enormous potential for scarves as headwear is bewildering when seen in the context of the mass of fabrics and patterns available for use. Both suitable fabrics and purchased scarves can be used for most of the ideas in this chapter. Purchased scarves come in every kind of fabric imaginable, from expensive pure silk to cheap and cheery cottons; Hermes scarves, Liberty squares, checked Burberry wools, red and white gypsy kerchiefs, and white miners' scarves are just a few of the many different types available.

The range of fabrics that can be made into scarves or scarf hats is just as wide. Almost any kind of material, print or plain, can be used, but avoid linen since it will crease easily, and fabrics that are too thick to drape or tie. Look out for the patterned fabrics which come specially printed for scarves with self borders already in the design. To help you pick an appropriate fabric for your chosen scarf look, some hints are given on the next page.

The different looks and effects that you can create with scarves are just as varied as the range of fabrics that they can be made from. You can tie, knot, twist, clip or sew scarves; double or treble them, and decorate in a mass of different ways; mix textures and colours in twists and braids; use more than one scarf; trim with ribbons and braids, decorative edgings, brooches and pins. Lots of exciting and original ideas for different scarf looks are given in this chapter.

Purchased scarves or fabrics can also be made up into permanently tied scarf hats. The scarf turbans on pages 44 and 45 can be made up quite easily from the flat patterns provided without the use of specialist equipment. In fact scarves can be used in any way you can imagine, showing that with thoughtful choice of fabric and styling, this versatile head accessory can create an immense number of fashion looks, ranging from the casual to the ultra-sophisticated.

Scarf Types

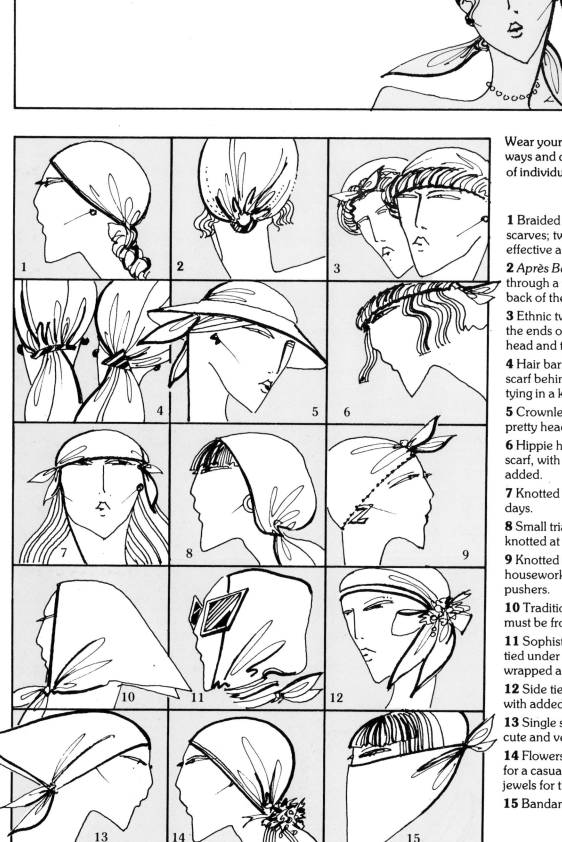

Wear your scarves in lots of different ways and create an exciting range of individual and effective looks.

1 Braided scarf tail with two scarves; two colours will look most effective and interesting.

2 *Après Bain* terrycloth scarf look through a plastic ring placed at the back of the neck.

3 Ethnic twist with two scarves or the ends of one twisted around the head and tied.

4 Hair barrette or brooch to hold a scarf behind the head, instead of tying in a knot.

5 Crownless brim worn over a pretty head scarf.

6 Hippie head band from a folded scarf, with another twisted one added.

7 Knotted handkerchief for sunny days.

8 Small triangular gypsy scarf knotted at the back.

9 Knotted in the front for housework, but better with pedal pushers.

10 Traditional horsey headscarf; must be from Hermes.

11 Sophisticated open tourer look, tied under the chin, scarf tails wrapped around the neck.

12 Side tied, dressed-up style, with added flower for formality.

13 Single small square, folded; cute and very young.

14 Flowers added to the back knot for a casual summer feel; do it with jewels for the evening.

15 Bandana for your get-away!

Scarf Fabrics

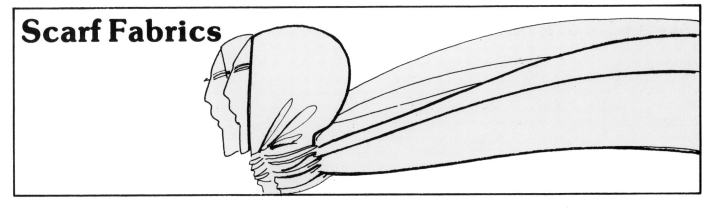

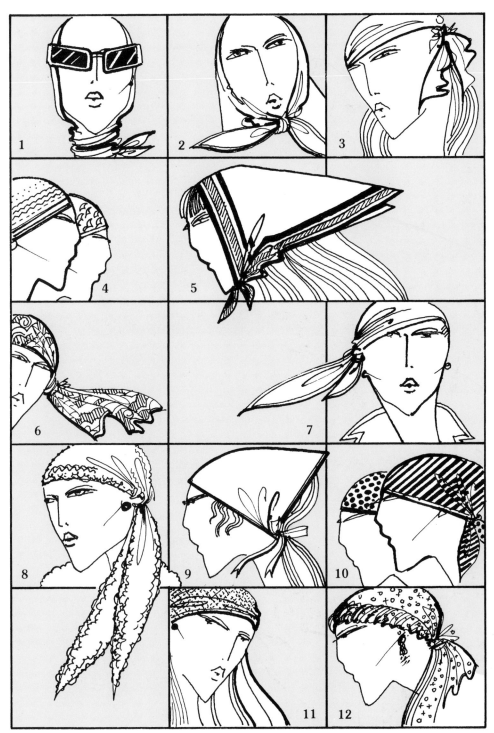

Use a wide variety of fabric types and textures for original scarf looks, but avoid those which are too thick to drape and tie.

1 Light crêpe jersey will drape and tie easily.

2 Plain silk for a glamorous look; a very fine silk like Honan works well while a twill type of silk will give more body.

3 Cheesecloth is more informal; it is stretchy and comes in a good range of colours.

4 Natural muslin, machine stitched or embroidered, will look original and interesting.

5 Cotton printed specially for scarves often comes with its own self border.

6 Silk foulard is very attractive in a lovely Liberty print.

7 Chiffon or georgette will float prettily in a breeze.

8 Lace comes in a wide range of patterns and designs - cut round the scallops or perhaps add a lace edging or border.

9 Plastic is possible, but end ties will need to be added to a fold-away rain hat.

10 Two cotton scarves stitched together to create an interesting reversible headscarf.

11 Light wool in different textures and weights will give a warmer, wintery feel.

12 Sequin covered chiffon for ultimate glitter.

Scarf Knots

Scarves can be worn in a mass of different ways, as is shown in this chapter. The knots involved in tying them are quite simple to master, if the diagrams given here are followed.

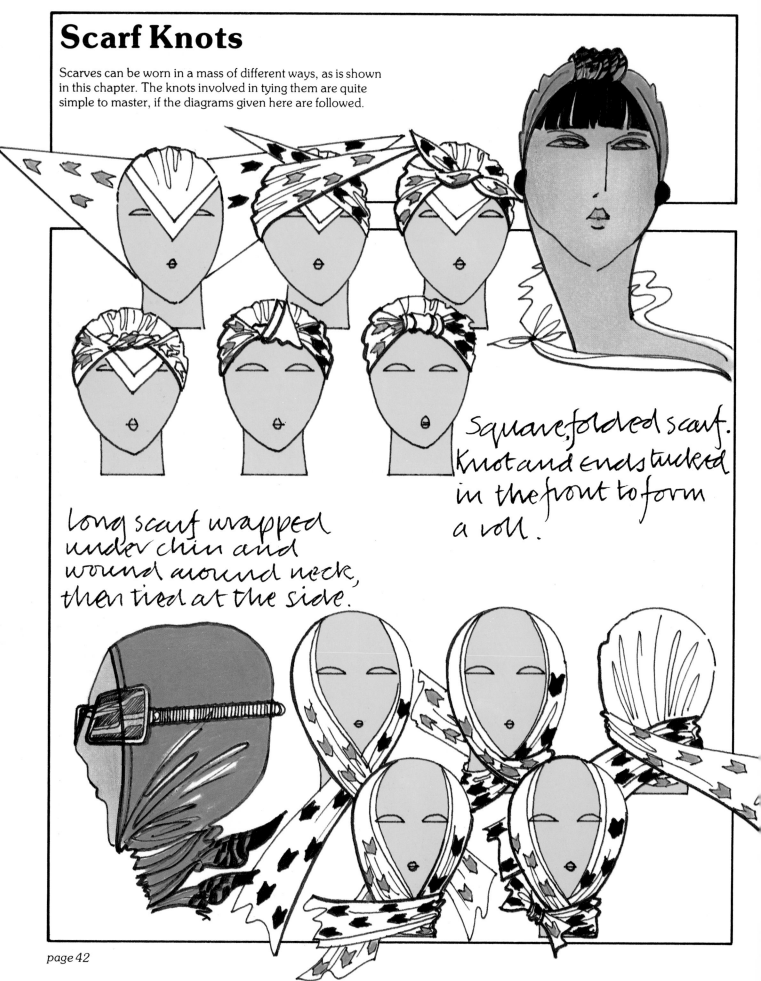

square, folded scarf. Knot and ends tucked in the front to form a roll.

long scarf wrapped under chin and wound around neck, then tied at the side.

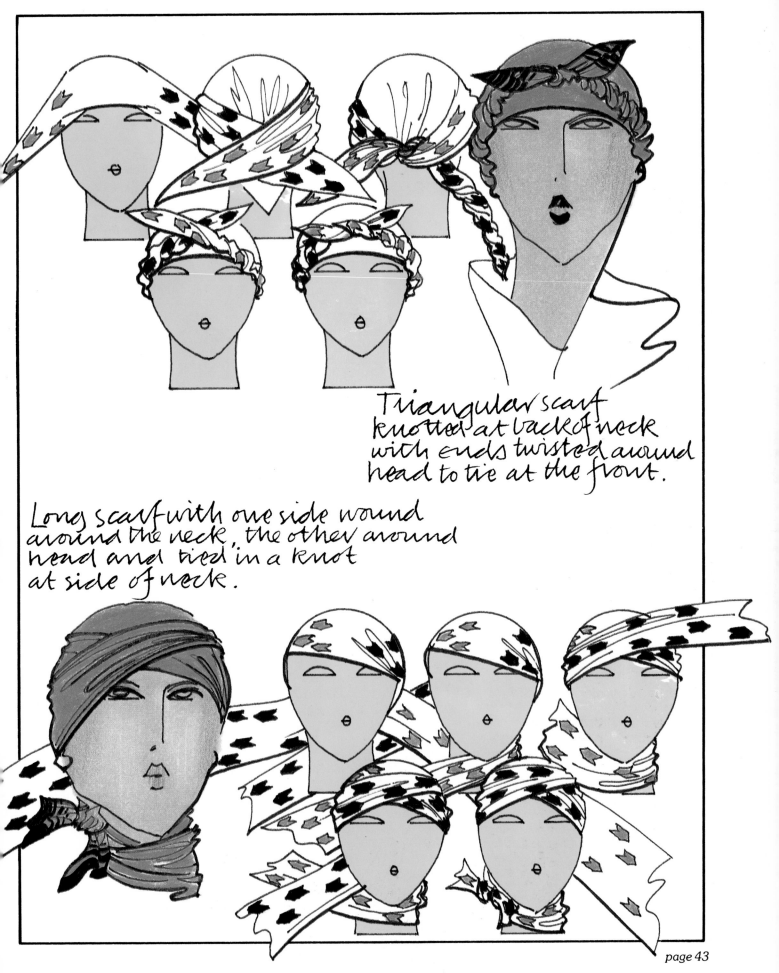

Triangular scarf knotted at back of neck with ends twisted around head to tie at the front.

Long scarf with one side wound around the neck, the other around head and tied in a knot at side of neck.

Scarf Turban with Pleated Back

Scarves can be tied in lots of different ways to achieve different looks, but you might like the idea of doing away with the need to re-tie a scarf every time you want to wear it. So make up a permanent scarf hat out of a favourite fabric or head square from this flat pattern; this scarf hat has a pleated back with short ties.

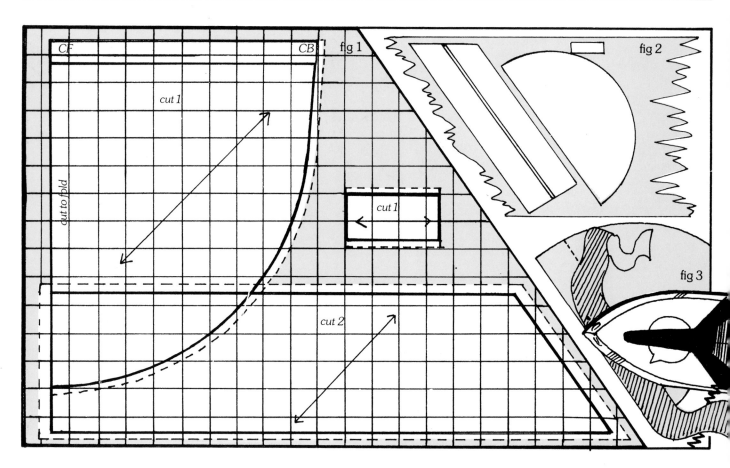

Materials
1 large head square or
60cm(⅝yd) light cotton or silk
35cm(⅜yd) dress weight iron-on interfacing
½m(½yd) organza for interfacing if silk is used for hat

Method
1 The pattern given is ¼ scale for a 57.2cm(22½in) head fitting (fig 1). Scale up on to graph paper all measurements except seam allowances ×4. For other head sizes see page 18.

2 Place scaled-up pattern on fabric following suggested lay (fig 2), and cut out fabric and interfacings on the cross.

3 To form the scarf crown, press iron-on interfacing along the crown head fitting (fig 3). If light silk is being used, mount fabric on to organza interfacing by zig-zag tacking all over; treat as one from now on.

4 Fold fabric over along edge of interfacing. Machine stitch along fabric edge (fig 4). Place fabric along headline of dolly.

5 Pin centre back seam towards the right side, and join only at interfaced part (fig 5). Arrange two pleats on each side of centre back. Pin pleats in at centre back. Work pleats from the outside towards the centre (fig 6). The centre piece will form a box pleat which will neaten the others.

6 To make the tie loop for the centre back, neaten tie by pressing over edges. Pin, then tack, centre tie on to the box pleat, right side to right side. Machine stitch over pleats and centre tie in one, along the head line. Roll centre tie over head fitting. Stitch centre tie inside hat at the head line to form a loop at the centre back.

7 To make scarf tie, fold tie lengthwise, right side to right side. Machine stitch all round leaving a 5cm to 7cm(2in to 3in) opening in the centre. Turn tie through, sew up opening with slip stitch and press. Insert tie through loop at centre back of hat, and either tie in a bow or leave free.

Scarf Turban with Gathered Back

Another attractive scarf turban that can be made by the flat pattern method has a gathered back and long ties. The ties make it quite an adaptable style of permanent scarf hat since they can be worn in so many different ways. Leave them flying at the back, tie them in a big floppy bow, wrap round your neck, or wind round your head and tie on the forehead.

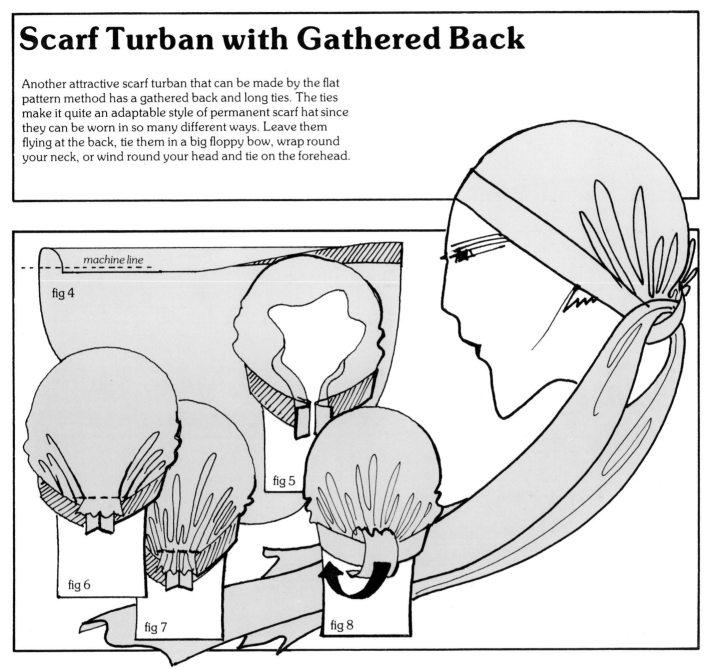

machine line

fig 4

fig 5

fig 6

fig 7

fig 8

Materials
1 large head square
1 long scarf or
¾m(¾yd) chosen fabric
35cm(⅜yd) dress weight iron-on interfacing

Method
1 The pattern given is ¼ scale for a 57.2cm(22½in) head fitting (fig 1). Scale up on to graph paper all measurements except seam allowances ×4. For other head sizes see page 18.

2 Place scaled-up pattern on fabric following suggested lay (fig 2) and cut out fabric and iron-on interfacing on the cross.

3 To form the scarf crown, iron interfacing along the crown head fitting. Fold fabric over along edge of interfacing. Machine stitch along fabric edge. Place fabric along headline of dolly.

4 Gather the back of the crown (fig 7). Machine stitch along the head line, attaching centre tie with same line of stitching.

Roll tie over head fitting and secure inside hat at head line to form loop at the centre back (fig 8).

5 To make scarf tie, fold tie lengthwise, right side to right side. Machine stitch all round leaving 5cm to 7cm(2in to 3in) opening in the centre. Turn tie through, slip stitch opening and press. Remember to make tie of double length to give long ends. Insert tie (or long ready-made scarf, if this is being used) through loop and arrange ends as required.

Scarf Looks and Trims

Scarves (whether bought or made from your own chosen fabric) are incredibly versatile and the number of different ways in which they can be tied and decorated is infinite. Here are some examples of the many ways in which they can be used, turning them from the commonplace into the thoughtful fashion accessory.

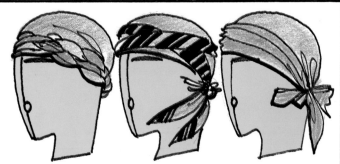

4 Mix different scarves by twisting one over the other. Alternate colours and textures, change patterns – stripes and spots, plain and print, glittery and plain for evening. Try tying a head band behind the neck over a head scarf.

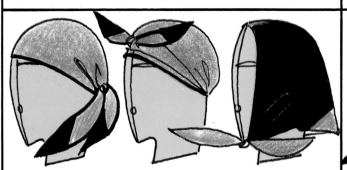

1 Tie your scarf behind your head and tuck in the ends for a purposeful look. Wrap the ends around your head (quite Arabian) or let them fall free.

5 Add a decorative edge in lace or ruffled self fabric by machine stitching to your scarf. Attach a strip of maribou, cock feathers or maribou mixture by hand, or if the occasion demands, even add strips of ostrich.

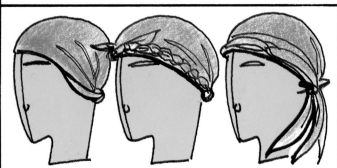

2 Give the corners of your scarf added colour by dyeing them or sewing on new corners; then tuck them in, wrap or dangle them. The change will be dramatic.

6 Sew baby ribbon on to the edges of a scarf. Satin, velvet, grosgrain and moiré ribbons are all available in a wide variety of colours. Sew both edges of ribbons on the flat either singly or in multiples of two or three.

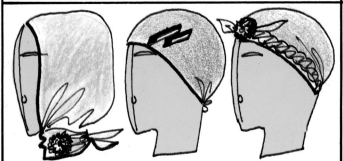

3 Trim plain head scarves with pins, brooches or badges. Place them in eye-catching positions, on scarf ties, or above forehead.

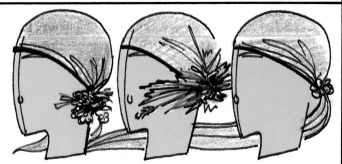

7 Attach different trimmings at the back of a tied scarf – flowers, natural grasses, feathers or even fresh flowers. Prepare a couple of extra ties to add to the original knot to create a longer back trim.

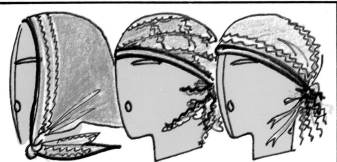

8 Appliqué rickrack, Russian braid, or lace edging all over mohair, jersey or cotton chintz scarves in checked or curved patterns, or use just a single line around the head fitting.

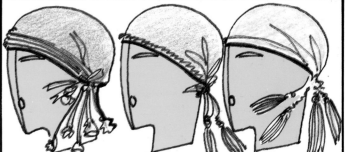

12 Make rouleaus to go round a scarf in self fabric, and put self fabric flowers or long or short tassels on the scarf ends. If you are using plain fabric, spray or dip the ends to give a shaded colour effect.

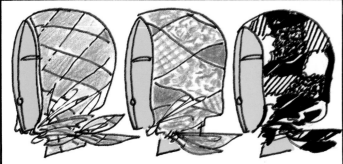

9 Make a scarf out of a patchwork of prints; traditional small florals are prettiest but plain colours look good too. Black and white never fails. Try combinations of different textures. In other words create your own fabric first.

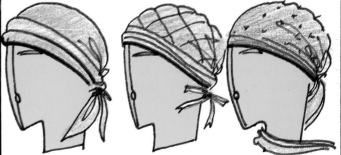

13 Quilt your scarf using a soft interfacing or batting. It will be warm, textured and original. Quilt in checks, lines or follow the pattern of the fabric design. Emphasize the pattern of the quilting with beads or French knots.

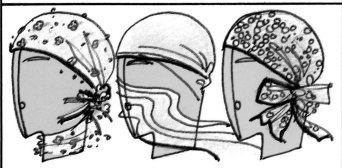

10 Sew tiny flowers on to organdy, sequins on to crêpe de Chine and jet beads on to taffeta and complete with similarly decorated trims or ties.

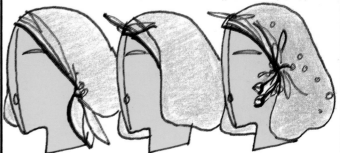

14 Tie a soft silk scarf up under your hair; wear this gypsy look with a fringed shawl – look the part by adding bells or beads as a trim.

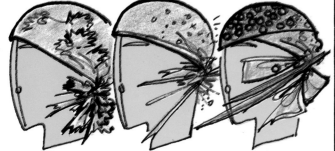

11 For really grand evenings try encrusted embroidered scarves trimmed with feathers, beads or silver; or gold lurex festooned with metal coloured beads or paillettes for larger than life trimmings.

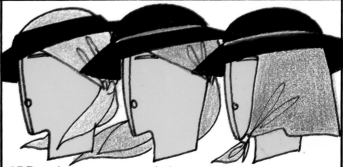

15 Put a hat over your scarf, show one through a crownless brim or attach one inside a hat. They all look good and can be practical too.

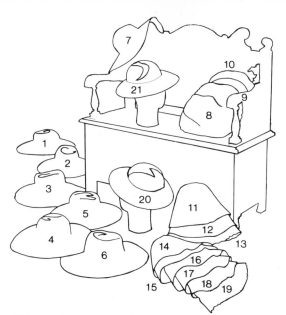

Felt Hood Types

1 Peach Bloom 2 Peach Bloom 3 Melusine 4 Peach Bloom
5 Plain felt 6 Plain felt 7 Double-sided Melusine 8 Peach Bloom
9 Peach Bloom 10 Peach Bloom 11 Velour 12 Velour 13 Velour
14 Velour 15 Velour 16 Fox Fur 17 Velour 18 Melusine
19 Melusine 20 Finished Peach Bloom hat
21 Finished Peach Bloom hat

Winter Felt Hats

Over the years felt has become one of the most important basic fabrics used in millinery manufacture. This is because of its natural ability to stretch and shrink when wet, and retain its shape when dry. These qualities make it an excellent material for hat making.

There are two types of felt, fur and wool. Both are produced by compressing wool or fur fibres. However, fur felt is infinitely superior and the home milliner would be well advised not to be seduced by the cheapness of wool felt, since the way it shrinks and its rather clumsy quality make it difficult to handle. Even altering or trimming ready-made hats in wool felt will be difficult.

For a long time felt manufacturers have produced semi-formed felt hat shapes which are known as 'hoods'. At this stage these preformed shapes resemble slightly the basic hats they will eventually be blocked into; they require a great deal of work on them before even a fitting is possible, let alone a styled shape. Hoods come in two shapes: the 'cone' for brimless or small brimmed hats and the 'capeline' for larger brimmed hats.

Felt hoods come in a comprehensive colour range since felt accepts dye readily. However, the dyeing process is very sophisticated and it is not advisable to attempt it at home. In addition, felts are available in a large number of finishes, which range from the normal smooth felt surface to the more fluffy finishes and beautiful velours with a velvet pile (this requires very delicate handling lest it mark). The variety of both colours and finishes come in basic hood shapes as well as in finished manufactured hats.

Felt hoods need to be blocked, and the basic procedures for this process are outlined on the next page; instructions are also given on how to make these blocked hoods into simple styles and on refurbishing and freshening up old hats. For those who do not wish to block their own hats, much of this chapter is devoted to exciting and original ideas and step-by-step instructions for altering and retrimming existing manufactured hats.

Blocking Felt Hoods

Methods of working in felt vary greatly within the millinery trade, and range from mass-produced hats made in their thousands on heavy plant on the one hand to those made in the model workroom producing only a few dozen or less of any given style.

The relatively inexpensive product found in most department stores is produced on hydraulically operated metal blocks which press out the hat from the hood in one piece, and which after a few finishing processes, is then ready for trimming. Model felts are blocked by hand on wooden blocks, using a cord or pins to hold the felt on the block while it dries, the crown and brim being dealt with separately. This latter technique is the one that the home hat maker will need to adopt.

Felt is a particularly stable material which will become totally malleable when steamed. It can then be pulled in any direction or over any shape while wet and pliable, and it will retain the new shape when it returns to its dry state. It has to be prevented from shrinking while it dries by pinning it, or by pulling tightly a cord in a groove around the edge of the block. However many of the blocks available to the general public are unlikely to come with such a groove, so 'T' pins are more practical for using at home.

The basic principles for blocking a new felt hood are set out here, together with instructions for assembling and finishing. The same techniques will apply whether you are using a capeline or a cone hood, or if you are adapting an existing hat. The instructions are for the simplest most common hat style but more advanced shapes can of course be tried and the same principles of blocking, joining, finishing and stiffening will apply.

Materials

A felt hood. Choose a cone for a small hat, a capeline for one with a larger brim
Grosgrain ribbon for head fitting and brim binding if required
Millinery wire for chosen brim size plus 10cm(4in) for overlap

Method

1 Dampen hood all over by steaming thoroughly.

2 Pull the hood down over crown block by taking hold of the brim and tugging very hard until the felt is tight over the crown (fig 1). Hold the felt down on the block with a spiral or by pinning with 'T' pins just below head line so as not to mark crown on the visible part of the finished hat (fig 2). The position of the head line is dependent on whether you choose a high or low crown.

3 Set the shape on the block by further steaming and pressing all over with a damp cloth and iron. Do not remove spiral or pins until the felt is thoroughly dry or it will immediately shrink.

4 Mark head line with pins and cut off brim below with a craft knife (fig 3). Take care not to stretch the blocked fitting.

5 Take the felt brim and shrink the centre hole until its circumference is slightly less than the head fitting required (fig 4). To achieve this, steam and pull the edge of the centre hole towards the centre, shrinking away the surplus under the iron and pressing cloth. You can also shape the outer brim to the approximate brim angle at this stage by the same method; it will mean less pulling on the block and will save time later on.

6 Pull shrunk circle over the brim block head fitting and then pull a grosgrain ribbon around the head fitting, pinning with 'T' pins every inch or so (fig 5).

7 Steam and pull out felt edge from the centre to the outer edge of block; pull evenly working alternately on one side and then on the other. This will prevent chasing fullness around the block. Pin bottom of brim well over edge of block to prevent marking the hat surface (fig 6). Wait until felt is dry and then cut brim edge according to what type of finish you wish to use. For a bound brim, cut brim bottom at the top of the block edge, but for a turned felt finish cut at the lower edge of block.

8 For a bound edge, wire brim edge by overcasting wire to brim starting at the centre back. For a turned edge slip stitch wire 1cm(⅜in) in from the edge (fig 7). Whichever way you choose, the wire must overlap at the centre back by at least 10cm(4in) and be well attached at the ends.

9 For a bound edge, bind edge of felt with 1.3cm(½in) grosgrain ribbon, matched to the colour of the hat or contrasting. For a turned finish, fold over edge of felt, lightly press with damp cloth and slip stitch down.

10 To join the crown to the brim match crown centre back to brim centre back and pin crown over brim. Sew together using large back stitch but sew round crown twice (fig 8).

11 Insert a 1.3cm(½in) grosgrain ribbon around head fitting and stab stitch into place (fig 9).

12 Most felts benefit from stiffening with a felt stiffening agent. This should be applied carefully to the finished hat working inside the crown and under the brim (fig 10). Take care not to apply the stiffener too liberally since it will cause the felt to shrink. In industrial manufacture the stiffener is applied to the hood prior to working on it and this method can also be used in hand work. However it will make the hood harder to handle while blocking though it will set well and eliminate the danger of shrinkage.

fig 1

fig 2

fig 3

fig 3

fig 4

fig 5

fig 6

fig 7

underbrim

fig 8

underbrim

underbrim

fig 9

fig 10

Trimming Felt Hats

The character of a basic plain felt hat (whether ready-made or blocked at home) can be altered dramatically by the use of different trimming ideas. If your chosen hat trim is then linked with other accessories, such as belts or bags, to emphasize the chosen trim, the fashion look of your whole outfit will be enhanced.

Many varied and inventive suggestions for trimming felt hats are given on the following pages but a detailed look at four different trim alternatives applied to the same original felt hat will give a good idea of the styling potential of this relatively small but crucial part of a hat.

1 If your coat or jacket is elegant but severe, brighten it up with a clip or brooch on the lapel or shoulder. The felt hat you might team with your outfit will look sharpened with a mirror image of the same pin. The clip or brooch may be merely pinned on to the hat, but it will make a hole which will show if you plan to vary the trim. Sewing, although more permanent, is a better method for attaching decorations of this kind. Experiment with using two ornaments, or three if they are small enough, and scatter or cluster them on the hat. Use plastic or precious metal, stick or kilt pins or earrings, and the juxtaposition of the clean, sharp metal or plastic, or the sheen of jewellery and the matte felt will be startling. Set above a clean tailored collar line which reflects the same image and doors will be opened for you!

2 Knitting yarn comes in an amazing range of textures and finishes and it has a natural affinity to felt, whether knitted up or used straight off the cone. Its flexibility makes it particularly suited to decorating the round surfaces of hats. Knitted hat trims can be made to match scarves, gloves and even sweaters and cardigans. It can be wound round felt

3 If you like wearing a scarf tied at the neck, cravat style, or loosely hung from one shoulder, why not nonchalantly tie a matching or deliberately contrasting scarf around your hat. Even if you tie a shawl around your waist, a hat trim can still be matched to it by twisting or knotting a printed, embroidered or fringed scarf around the crown. Whether it is single or double, just tie it naturally. Add a few tacks for security and finish the trim off by adding a pin or soft rouleau for a casual relaxed look.

4 Both dog leads and collars, and all sorts of webbing and leather belts and straps are perfect for trimming felt hats and give the sportiest of 'hunting and shooting' country looks. Buckle, stitch or tie your chosen strap around the hat and link it by colour and fastening type to fishing or shooting shoulder bags, luggage or umbrella straps. Buy two belts and use one at the waist and one on your hat. Take a long strap and wind it twice round the hat; it will sit nicely on the crown and only needs a secret stitch or two to hold it secure. Put on your tweeds and brogues and you will be ready to stride out into the countryside.

hats, ribbed, embroidered, or twisted in bouclé wool, fluffy angoras or shiny rayons. Link a knit trim to a fisherman's sweater by using an Aran cable as a head band or make your felt shimmer with lurex yarn saddle stitched over the crown, to go with a glittery knitted sweater – and leave your hat on when dining out for an added air of mystery.

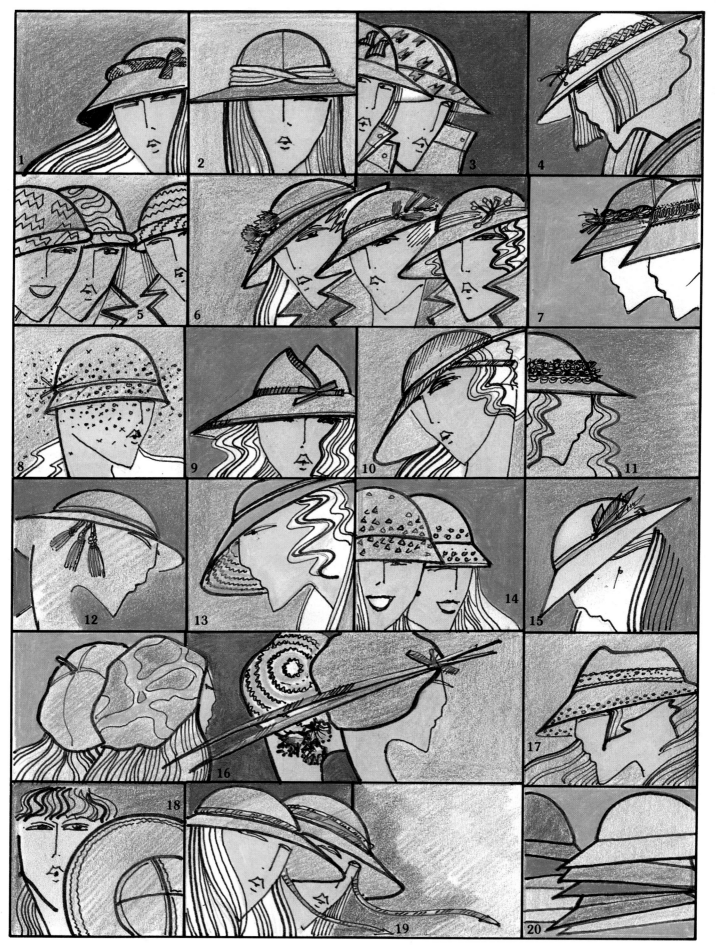

More Decorative Trims for Felts

Because of the prohibitive cost of hand work, most factory-made hats are usually trimmed in a very basic way, and what trims are provided are rarely well attached. However if you feel the original trims are not very fashionable, or individual and interesting enough, they can easily be removed. An odd flower or bunch of cherries is readily parted from its hat by snipping a few stitches and erasing any marks left by lightly steaming and brushing. You will then be ready to experiment with you own choice of trim. Use any of the following ideas or design your own, but keep them simple and effective and always neat. Try to be witty with them, but not too flamboyant. All the suggestions given here can be used to decorate or finish off a felt you have blocked yourself or a ready-made hat.

1 Silk or wool rouleaus of padded fabric contrast well with a matte felt. Use one or two thick rolls or several thin ones as a head band. Cut the fabric on the cross and stuff the rolls with wadding or batting.

2 Rouleaus of your dress or scarf fabric can be pulled round the crown of your hat, and twisted at the front or side like a skein of wool. Remember to cut the fabric on the cross, and try adding a piped cord.

3 Pieces of leather cut into shapes and glued on to your felt hat can look very effective. Shapes can also be appliquéd on to the brim by zig-zag machine stitch, but not on to the crown as it will not go under a domestic sewing machine. Repeat a small pattern or use a single more dramatic shape.

4 Braid some leather thongs to use as a head band. Try three, five or even seven braids if you can handle them. Experiment with different widths and colour combinations; thread some small beads on to the thongs as you go.

5 If you have an old felt hat you do not wear any more you could cut it up and use the pieces to trim a new one. Design a relief pattern – a pinked head band and smaller matched pinked pieces to scatter over the whole hat, for example. Glue on the pieces and remember that toning colours often look even better than contrasting ones.

6 Knitting wool trims can be used in many different ways. Pompons, fringed tassels, plain winds and knitting wool embroidery will all look good on felt hats.

7 Most braids, particularly furnishing trimmings for lampshades and curtains, have silky finishes which contrast beautifully with felt surfaces. They come in hundreds of colours and patterns.

8 Veiling can be a lovely trim for felts but use heavier grades for winter hats. You will have difficulty in finding silk veiling nowadays but a good man-made one is quite acceptable. Use one with a dot pattern, and always add a small rouleau or a ribbon head band to hide the back stitch you will need to use to control the veil gathering around the crown.

9 If you decide to add grosgrain ribbon, the most widely used hat finish of all for both women's and men's hats, to your felt, do not be content just to put a plain ribbon around the crown. Bind the edges, fold it, make rosettes, bows or loops

out of it – it is a much more versatile ribbon than people think. You can try all the same tricks with velvet and satin ribbon. All ribbons come in lots of colours and widths.

10 An underbrim strap or band can give a smart stylish look and it will be needed if your hat has a very shallow crown which does not sit comfortably on the head. It will look good as well as giving that bit of extra security.

11 Metal finishes can look spectacular on a felt hat. Chains, shoe trimmings and all sorts of metal fastenings in both gold and silver can be added to the head line or scattered all over the hat. Gold and silver look best on darker colours, but watch their weight and do not overload the hat.

12 Trims need not always be placed on the top surface of a hat; underbrim decoration can be subtle and sophisticated. Try hanging tassels from the head fitting at the back or side.

13 Rickrack applied in concentric circles on the underside of the brim can give a hidden quality to an apparently plain hat – the millinery equivalent of the mink-lined raincoat!

14 Studding felt is very effective and works well, since it is thick enough to disguise the claws that hold the studs secure and it prevents them showing underneath. Pyramid studs, stars and squares are all available in gold and silver, and can be arranged in attractive patterns.

15 Make a cluster of feathers, bind them together with fine wire and sew on to the side of your head band. Use feathers of different colours, with different markings, long, short or spiky ones. You can colour them yourself with markers.

16 Felt berets seldom come with trimmings apart from the traditional stalk on top, so why not add pompons in knitting wool, pin on a pheasant feather or embroider with lurex thread. You could even buy two berets and combine them by cutting out shapes from each and re-jigsawing them together. You will then have two patterned berets in different colours.

17 Punching holes in felt with a belt punch is very effective, since clean holes can be made. The punch will only reach the first inch of the outside brim so design a pattern to go around the edge. You can punch the pattern on the crown as well, if you are prepared to cut it off and then reassemble the hat after punching.

18 Stitch your brim all over with button hole thread in different colours; if you have an embroidery attachment on your sewing machine it can be used to great effect. Use large stitches otherwise the felt will perforate like postage stamps and thus tear easily.

19 Cord or rope can be knotted in lots of different ways to decorate a felt hat. Dressing-gown tassels or laces with metal tags (as on Texan string ties) will finish off the ends nicely.

20 Do not forget that the decision not to add a trim is perfectly valid, so the final suggestion might well be to leave your felt hat perfectly plain.

Grosgrain Head Band and Tailored Bow Trim

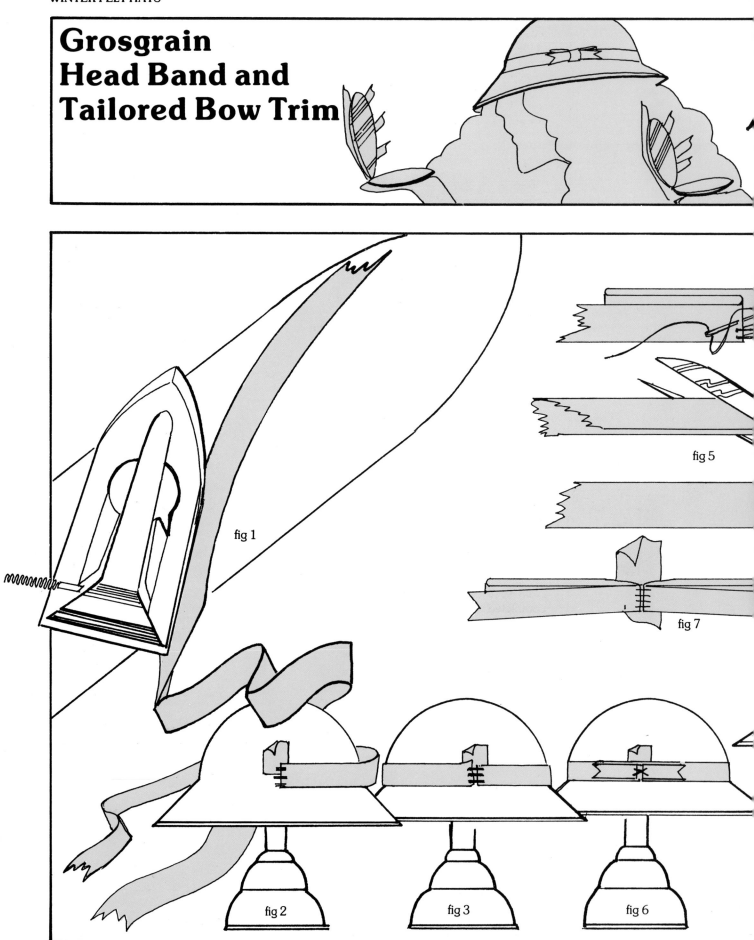

fig 1

fig 5

fig 7

fig 2

fig 3

fig 6

Although grosgrain ribbon is one of the most frequently used hat trims, it is also one of the most effective. Since it curves well, it is easy to work with and it comes in a variety of widths and colours. Try out the trim given here for a crisp, tailored look or wrap, braid or buckle it like one of the alternatives on the right.

Materials
A purchased or self-blocked felt hat 100cm(40in) grosgrain ribbon, either 1.3cm(½in), 2.5cm(1in) or 3.8cm(1½in) wide. If possible use French ribbon since it is of superior quality, but it is not always available

Method
1 From the ribbon cut a 59.7cm(23½in) head band; this includes 2.5cm(1in) for seam allowances. Also cut 30.5cm(12in) for the bow and 9cm(3½in) for the tie to go over the bow.

2 Curve the head band ribbon under the iron by stretching one edge; the more sloped the crown, the more the ribbon will need to be curved (fig 1).

3 With two or three stab stitches attach both tie-over and one end of the head band to the side of the hat (fig 2). Place the curved edge of the head band ribbon against the brim.

4 Place head band round the head line and stab stitch firmly in position (fig 3).

5 Prepare bow out of 30.5cm(12in) ribbon already cut (fig 4). Cut fishtails on the ends of the bow by folding ribbon ends over and cutting at a 45° angle (fig 5). Place completed bow in position on the head band and join by stab stitching it down firmly (fig 6).

6 Roll the previously attached tie over the bow (fig 7), and tuck it under the head ribbon to hide previous stitching and joins. Use a couple of invisible stitches to keep it in place.

7 Finally, stab stitch the bottom of the head band ribbon all round the hat to prevent it riding up.

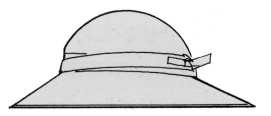

Wrap ribbon round crown twice and finish the trim off with a neat knot.

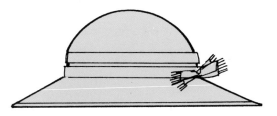

Use two parallel head bands in contrasting or similar colours, and finish knot by fringing ends.

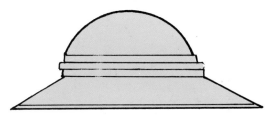

Emphasize a wide head band by adding a narrower ribbon to it in a different or toning colour.

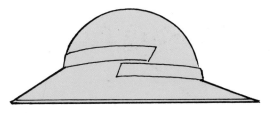

Overlap a head band for a clean cut and interestingly different geometric effect.

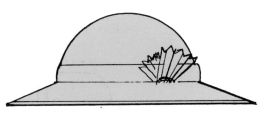

Add a rosette of pleated ribbon for a crisp and interesting trim.

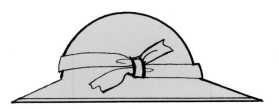

Pull together an overlapped head band with a tie, and finish it off with a knot.

Draped Scarf or Fabric Trim

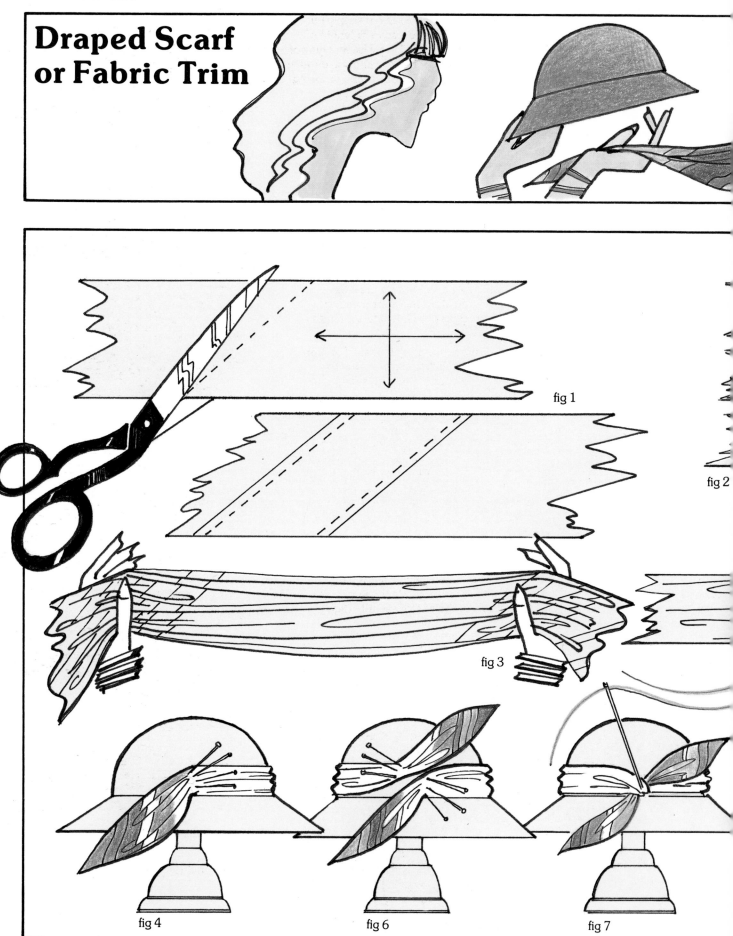

fig 1

fig 2

fig 3

fig 4

fig 6

fig 7

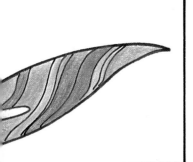

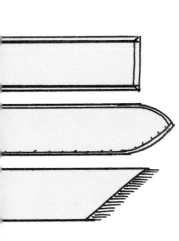

Another way to trim a felt hat simply but effectively is to drape a scarf or length of fabric around the headline. Use any type of material as long as it is light and soft enough to drape well. Try out contrasting or toning colours, and vary the basic look by threading fabric through rings or buckles, or by using two scarves side by side or twisted together.

Materials
A purchased or self-blocked felt hat
A long scarf or
75cm(30in) length of chosen fabric.
Cotton, light wool or silk will drape well

Method
1 If using fabric, cut out on the cross, leaving seam allowances for rolled or hemmed edges (fig 1). Cut fabric about 30.5cm(12in) wide.

2 Ascertain perfect length of scarf or fabric by having a trial drape around the hat. Prepare the ends of the trim, straight, curved or cross cut (fig 2). If you are using silk, roll the edges; machine hem the edges if the fabric is cotton; fringe if it is wool.

3 Drape fabric around the headline of the hat by gathering it through your fingers (fig 3) and pinning it directly on to the side of the hat (fig 4). It is important to pin drapes in order to see the effect before sewing permanently. Stab stitch the draped fabric to the hat. If you find handling the fabric difficult, use a gathering stitch (fig 5).

4 Pin one end of the fabric in a position from which a knot can be started (fig 6). Stab stitch to the hat. Tie the knot and sew it invisibly to the hat for security (fig 7).

fig 5

Two scarves side by side.

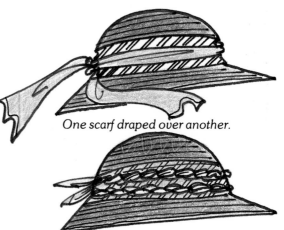

One scarf draped over another.

Twisted scarf over a plain draped one.

Hat over headscarf.

Two scarves twisted together.

Scarf through ring or buckle.

Knitting Yarn
Twist and
Tassel Trim

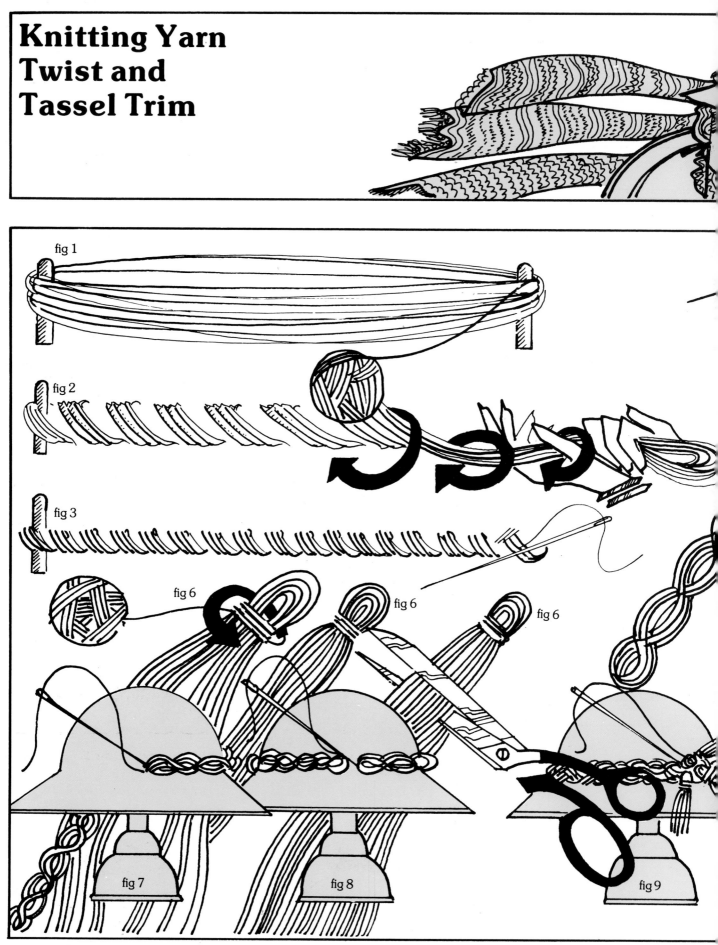

fig 1

fig 2

fig 3

fig 6

fig 6

fig 6

fig 7

fig 8

fig 9

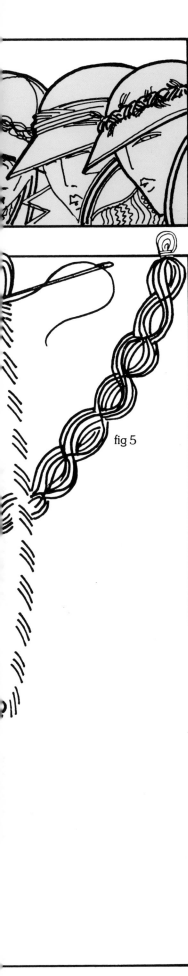

fig 5

Knitting yarn textures complement felt finishes beautifully and the combination will result in a warm wintery look, especially if the twist and tassel trim is matched to scarf and gloves. Use heavier weights of wool for best results; finer plys need more yarn in the twists and this will increase the overall elasticity which can sometimes buckle a blocked crown.

Materials

A purchased or self-blocked felt hat
One ball of ordinary knitting wool 3, 4 or 5 ply

Method

1 To make the knitting yarn twist unwind your wool into a skein approximately two and a quarter times your head measurement (fig 1). From one end twist the skein until it is quite tight (fig 2).

2 Overcast one end of the twisted skein with the same yarn and a darning needle to prevent it from unravelling (fig 3).

3 Put one end of the twist to the other and secure with stitches of wool (fig 4). Release tension from other end and skein will twist into an attractive braid (fig 5).

4 To prepare the two tassels double over about ten 18cm(7in) lengths of wool. Bind them tightly together in wool about 1.3cm(½in) from one end. Trim off other end to form a 6.5cm(2½in) tassel (fig 6). Repeat this process for a second or third.

5 To attach trim to hat, tack one end of the twist to the side of the hat (fig 7). Pull twist round hat and tack other end to hat, matching up edges of braid (fig 8). Stab stitch the two or three tassels over the meeting point to disguise it (fig 9).

Wind yarn round crown and decorate with small wool tassels placed at random.

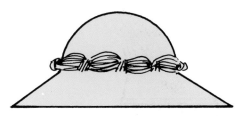

Wrap yarn round crown and tie over with wool at intervals.

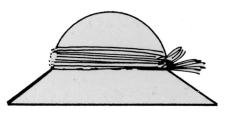

Wrap yarn round the crown, tie, and cut ends to form a fringed trim.

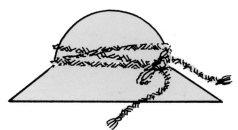

Plait or braid yarn in different colours and textures, and wind round the crown.

Join the two ends of a yarn twist with a plastic or metal ring.

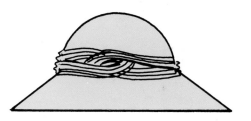

Loop two ends of yarn through one another to form a neat trim.

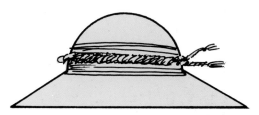

Place a thin yarn twist over a differently coloured or textured plain yarn wind.

page 61

Fashion Looks

Link up winter felt hats to your wardrobe by careful choice of colours and co-ordinating trims. Make them as smart or as casual as you like but keep the trims neat and crisp.

Twist yarn around the crown of a felt hat to team up with a thick warm sweater.

For a sleek winter look appliqué punched felt strips to a felt hat to echo the pinked pattern on a leather coat.

Co-ordinate criss-cross stitching on a head band and brim edge of hat with criss-cross quilting on a coat collar.

e a studded head
nd to keep a felt
t as tough looking
as a chic jacket.

A helmet shaped
felt is the only
hat for an all
in one stying
suit.

Link up
leather
strap hat trim
with bag, belts
and other leather
accessories.

Simple Turbans

Of all the basic hat types, the turban with its organized rich folds and snug fit, is perhaps the most elegant. Totally covering the head and worn well down over the ears its slick severity will give a real air of sophistication. Do not feel that it will only suit a particular type of face, since by controlling its silhouette by draping and by using an infinitely variable headline, the turban can be easily adapted to look good on a wide variety of different face shapes.

The most sophisticated and comfortable turbans are those that are totally soft. The final look achieved by draping onto a soft base of tarlatan or rayon net is the most normal, but the making needs to be extremely skillful. Although harder turbans look more sculpted on their stiff net shapes, such as blocking net, this is probably the type to start with as the stiff base will allow you more control of the fabric.

With turban making a whole range of light unstructured fabrics, many unsuitable for other types of millinery, becomes available: chiffon, organza, sequin covered georgette, the lightest silk, and very fine jerseys, all fabrics that will open up the possibilities of late day hat wearing. The turban really comes into its own in the evening, for the range of evening wear possibilities are multiplied many times on account of the comparative lack of blocking required.

In this chapter methods for blocking simple turban shapes are described together with some easy to handle draping techniques and trimming possibilities. Limber up your fingers since draping will require them to be nimble; it is not easy to control the fabric but it can be mastered with practice. And remember to wear your turban confidently. It is not a hat for perching on the back of the head; so pull it down well over the ears to cover the hair.

Turban Fabrics and Turban Types

As in other forms of millinery, the general rule of lightness still applies when choosing fabric for a draped hat. Very heavy fabrics should be avoided, though bulky materials do not have to be totally excluded, since the number of folds, and thus the amount of fabric, can be controlled. Stiff fabrics like taffeta, stiff cotton and gabardine should be left well alone as they are too brittle to drape well. However since it is not always necessary to block turbans, man-made fabrics can sometimes be used.

Whatever fabric you decide to use for a turban, remember that it must always be cut on the true bias; if it is even slightly off grain the draping will not fold cleanly and the folds will break and pucker. This even includes jersey, though if you are very short on fabric you can try using it on the straight; for the perfectionist however, cutting this fabric on the cross gives far better results. The turbans illustrated here show the range of fabrics that work well and some of the different styles turbans can be made in.

1 Wool jersey turban with a tight front and alternately lapped folds.

2 Hurel jersey with soft folds beneath the head line for a soft and slightly stretchy ear covering and fitting.

3 Front trimmed mohair with just a few soft drapes for a light and warm effect.

4 Both Banlon and knitted rayon drape well but need more stitching as they can not be set by light steaming.

5 Terrycloth and cotton jersey – the nearest the formal turban gets to being sporty.

6 Cotton pulled to the front is young and chic. Wear it with a blouse and jeans.

7 Head band only, but made up on a base net which keeps it more formal.

8 Print or plain chiffon with lots of fine drapes using a great deal of fabric but remaining light and elegant.

9 Side draped foulard silk, draped to both sides and trimmed, can look much younger.

10 Glitter encrusted chiffon, sleek and tight, sparkly and lightweight, is splendid with high necks and slinky long-sleeved dresses.

11 Damask Poiret style turban with loose, bulky folds looks very theatrical. Pad out folds with fleecy batting which is light and soft.

12 Sequin covered fabrics are soft and pliable – perfect for parties and grand occasions.

13 Even leather will pull into shape if it is soft. Keep it neat with few folds and it will be very effective.

14 Crêpe de Chine pulled round to the back with fine pleats for a truly elegant and light appearance.

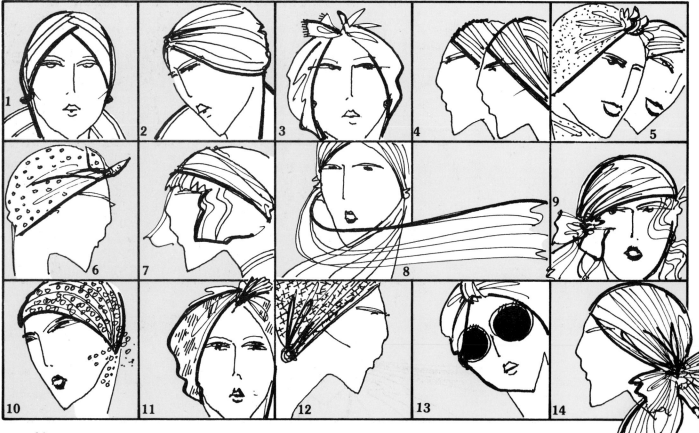

Trimming Turbans

Whether you have bought yourself a basic ready-made turban or have blocked and draped one yourself, following the instructions on page 68, you might like the idea of adding an appropriate trim to give it that extra lift. Of course the draping may look interesting enough in itself so that no further decorative features are needed.

On many draped styles, however, trimmings can often act as camouflage for unfinished ends on side, front or back, so they can often serve a functional, as well as decorative, purpose. As with other types of hat, a wide variety of trim ideas can be used, and some suggestions are listed here.

1 Tie a giant knot in jersey at the back of a turban. It will hide the ends of the gathering and make an attractive low centre back feature.

2 On a chiffon draped style float long ends from one side for a romantic look when flying out behind. Or attach the ends at the centre back and wrap them around the neck two or three times.

3 Add flowers where the turban folds converge. Use bought artificial flowers or make them yourself (*see* page 110) and try them in self or contrasting colours. Place small rouleaus round the trimming for a pretty finish.

4 When draping in tweed, gather a few soft folds into the front, and then hold them together with ornamental hair decorations or men's tie pins.

5 Decorate a silk turban with ostrich pompons placed at the side. Knitting wool pompons can be used on jersey for a less exotic look.

6 Pepper the turban with flowers over white or cream organza for a bride. Try matching or contrasting flowers on brighter colours for other occasions.

7 Run silk cords or satin ribbons along the folded part of the drapes and trim ends with tassels. Use fine leather rouleaus along Donegal tweed drapes and tie ends into knots or finish off with bootlace tags.

8 If draping from the back, knot the front or over wrap it with a centre tie on soft crêpe hats.

9 Add a stand-up trim in pleated or stiffened fabric as a centre front trim. Very sculptured, very formal.

10 Attach feathers to any part of the turban – front, back, sides or arrange attractively at interesting angles at any point on the hat.

Blocking and Draping a Turban

To create a really successful turban it is necessary first to prepare a blocked
net base to give the hat more body and to make the draping of the fabric
easier to handle. The procedure for blocking a net base, and then draping a
head hugging turban in light wool is described here, and it can easily be
adapted to suit different shapes and fabrics.

fig 1

fig 2

fig 3

fig 4

fig 5

fig 6

fig 7

fig 8

fig 9

fig 10

fig 11

fig 12

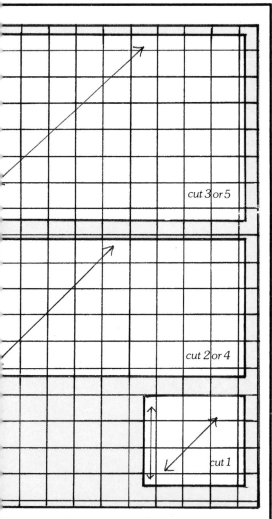

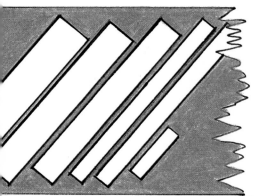

Blocking the Net Base

Materials
½m(½yd) blocking net in a colour close to that of your chosen fabric
Piece of clear plastic film

Method
1 Cover dolly totally with a piece of plastic film to prevent the net sticking to the canvas dolly. Pin it under bottom of dolly, pulling it down tightly so as to remove any wrinkles.

2 Fold the blocking net double and from it cut a 45cm(18in) square. Soften the net square in steam and pull down over the dolly. Pin down the corners into side of dolly with drawing pins (fig 1). As you pull it down, continue to steam it; it will tear easily if you do not keep it damp.

3 Pull out most of the gathers until nearly smooth and then spring a spiral over net. Continue pulling net from under spiral until all fullness has been pulled away (fig 2). Cut away surplus net from bottom and allow net to dry. When it is completely dry, remove spiral.

4 Tack your chosen head line on to the net. Turn back net to head line and press with a cool iron, but not on exact edge of head line, which is best left rolled rather than creased. Cut turnback to a neat 1.3cm(½in) seam allowance (fig 3).

5 Loosen net shape from dolly, and pull off.

Draping the Turban

Materials
¾m(¾yd) light wool
½m(½yd) fleecy batting
Grosgrain ribbon for head fitting
Blocked net base

Method
1 The pattern given is ¼ scale for a 57.2cm(22½in) head fitting. Scale up on to graph paper all measurements except seam allowances ×4 (fig 4). Place scaled up pattern on fabric following suggested lay and cut out on the cross. Cut strips for drapes 33cm(13in) long. Make them up to 20.3cm(8in) wide, or as little as 7.5cm(3in) according to taste. Use a few wide strips for soft easy draping, narrower ones for tight organized folds (fig 5).

2 Take crossway strip of fabric plus seam allowances for the head fitting binding. Underline with similar strip of fleecy batting by zig-zag tacking. Pull head fitting binding round edge of net shape, right side to net. Pin up centre back seam. Pin, tack and then machine stitch in position (fig 6). Pin and then tack other edge of binding right round and right through net base (fig 7).

3 Return bound net shape to dolly. Take a wide crossway strip of fabric and cover top of crown, pulling and gathering from centre front to centre back (fig 8). Attach at either end.

4 Take centre tie and gather. Attach it to back of turban above stitching of first drape through the fabric to the net (fig 9).

5 Take each strip of fabric in turn, fold in half lengthways and attach end to cover centre front of turban. Pull round turban to centre back. Gather and attach at back. Continue to add strips working alternately on either side, each strip covering stitching of previous one (fig 10).

6 Last two strips must have folds on both sides. Attach them to turban inside head fitting to hide previous stitches. Pull from centre front to centre back, gather and attach (fig 11). Roll over centre tie and attach inside head fitting (fig 12). Secure draped strips to net with occasional stab stitches beneath drapes, working from inside.

7 Insert a shaped grosgrain ribbon inside head fitting, slip stitching it to the original binding to hide raw edge.

Turban Variations

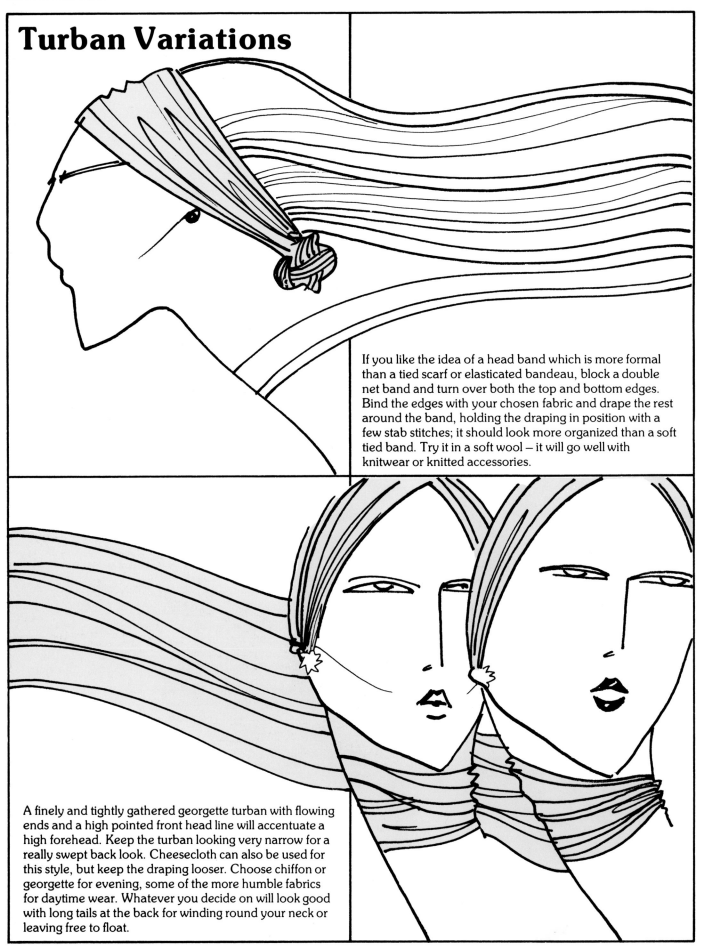

If you like the idea of a head band which is more formal than a tied scarf or elasticated bandeau, block a double net band and turn over both the top and bottom edges. Bind the edges with your chosen fabric and drape the rest around the band, holding the draping in position with a few stab stitches; it should look more organized than a soft tied band. Try it in a soft wool – it will go well with knitwear or knitted accessories.

A finely and tightly gathered georgette turban with flowing ends and a high pointed front head line will accentuate a high forehead. Keep the turban looking very narrow for a really swept back look. Cheesecloth can also be used for this style, but keep the draping looser. Choose chiffon or georgette for evening, some of the more humble fabrics for daytime wear. Whatever you decide on will look good with long tails at the back for winding round your neck or leaving free to float.

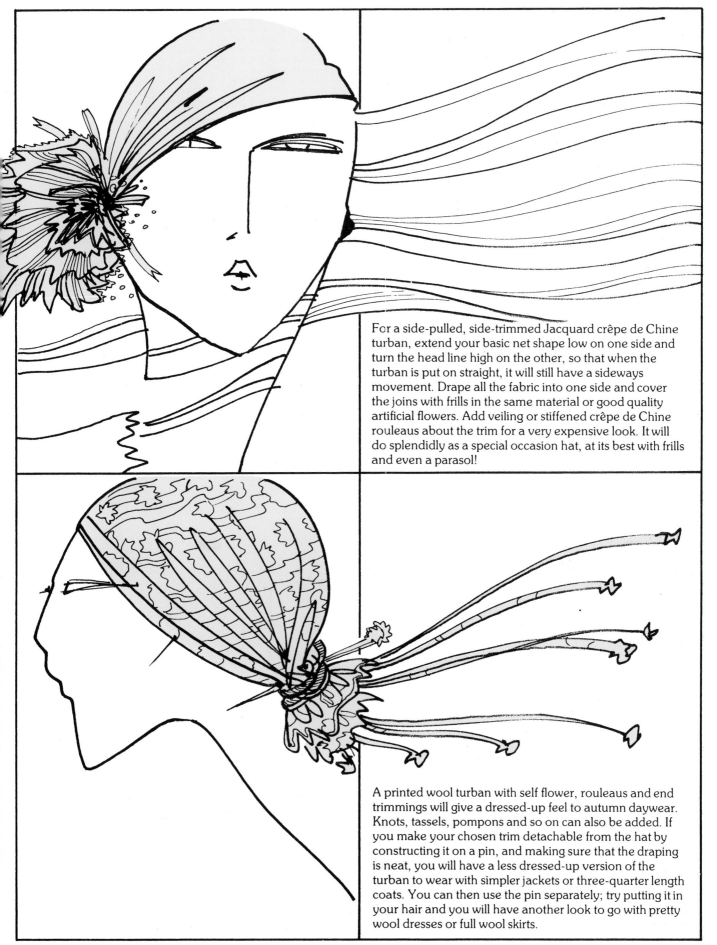

For a side-pulled, side-trimmed Jacquard crêpe de Chine turban, extend your basic net shape low on one side and turn the head line high on the other, so that when the turban is put on straight, it will still have a sideways movement. Drape all the fabric into one side and cover the joins with frills in the same material or good quality artificial flowers. Add veiling or stiffened crêpe de Chine rouleaus about the trim for a very expensive look. It will do splendidly as a special occasion hat, at its best with frills and even a parasol!

A printed wool turban with self flower, rouleaus and end trimmings will give a dressed-up feel to autumn daywear. Knots, tassels, pompons and so on can also be added. If you make your chosen trim detachable from the hat by constructing it on a pin, and making sure that the draping is neat, you will have a less dressed-up version of the turban to wear with simpler jackets or three-quarter length coats. You can then use the pin separately; try putting it in your hair and you will have another look to go with pretty wool dresses or full wool skirts.

Summer Straw Hats

Straw is another of millinery's most popular basic materials and it is to the spring and summer seasons what felt is to the autumn and winter. It is so commonly used in hat making that it is woven into preformed hat shapes which are called 'hoods' as they are in felt and again they come in two basic forms, the cone and the capeline.

Like felt but to a lesser degree straw has a flexibility that makes it suitable for blocking. It will stretch and shrink but more effort is needed when using tightly woven hoods, to pull it into shape. A good deal of ironing and steaming to maintain the shape is also required, but it will be well worth the effort since straw makes up into the lightest, crispest and most attractive summer hats and it will look soft or sharp, delicate or tailored according to taste.

Nowadays straw hoods come mostly from China and other Far Eastern countries – very fine straws from Switzerland are now extremely expensive – and are available in an array of finishes described by exotic names. Synthetic straw is widely used and piece straw and a strip straw can also be bought, though the latter tends to make up into rather clumsy hats, and the often interesting textures it contains are usually pressed out when it is steamed and ironed.

Sadly the colours in which straws are nowadays available are rather limited, due mostly to the poor range promoted by the millinery trade each season. Dyeing services do exist, but can only be used for bulk orders. You can, however, colour a straw hood with proprietary dyes, but only attempt to tint it rather than to change the colour totally.

Described on the next page are the basic principles for blocking straw hoods. Decorate your chosen straw hat using the step-by-step instructions in this chapter or experiment with some of the mass of other inventive and effective ideas also shown. Mix and match with outfits in cool cottons and soft silks for the sunniest of summer looks.

Straw Hood Types
1 *Pari-sisal*   2 *Sisal*   3 *Sisal*   4 *Sisal*   5 *Pari-sisal*   6 *Sisal*
7 *Nutmeg*   8 *Baku*   9 *Paper Panama*   10 *Panamalac*   11 *Racello*
12 *Jungle Cane*   13 *Fancy Bao*   14 *Fancy Bao*   15 *Fancy Sisal*
16 *Panama*   17 *Fancy Bao*   18 *Xian*   19 *Finished Sisal hat*
20 *Finished Sisal hat*

Blocking Straw Hoods

Although the processes involved are different, mass-produced straw hats have a lot in common with mass-produced felts. Like felts, raw straw hoods (both cones and capelines) are treated to a mixture of heat, steam and pressure to force them into the shape of the metal blocks. Dampening, stretching and drying all take place in one operation, and although a little hand pressing may sometimes be called for, the hat is practically finished in one movement. Only the edge finishing, stiffening and trimming need to be completed by hand.

In model millinery hand-blocked hoods require 'panning'. This means that the hood has to be pressed smooth on a metal block to give a finish to the rough woven product. This roughness is hard to remove at home by hand on wooden blocks, but the home milliner can easily purchase smooth straws, like Pari-buntal or -sisal, from a wholesaler which are already panned.

Straw hoods can be stretched after dampening with a cloth, but the wet heat produced by steaming them will make pulling easier for the home hat-maker. The drying time will also be lessened, but as with felts, care must be taken not to remove the hood from the block before it has dried thoroughly. Polishing the straw with the iron will help to dry it and to set the shape. The shine imparted during this process is the mark of an expensive hand-made hat, and is entirely different from a gloss effect of varnish only.

The principles for blocking a new Pari-sisal capeline hood are given here, together with instructions for assembling and finishing off the hat. These methods can also be adopted when altering or adapting an existing hat. If a textured straw is to be used, the system remains the same, but care must be taken to prevent fraying. A line of machine stitching along the cut sections will prevent this happening, and remember that only the lightest of pressing is permissible on textured straws.

Materials
A smooth straw capeline hood
Millinery wire to brim measurement plus 10.2cm(4in) for overlap
Grosgrain ribbon for head fitting

Method
1 Dampen hood from inside with wet rag. Keep tea kettle on boil as additional steaming and dampening will be necessary as you continue to work.

2 Centre woven middle of hood crown on crown block; pull crown down hard by pulling the brim, taking care not to crease panned brim (fig 1). Spring spiral over straw crown, placing it just below planned head line so as not to mark the actual hat (fig 2). Pull hood along the grain from under spiral

fig 1   fig 2   fig 3   fig 4

fig 5   fig 6   fig 7

until it is totally smooth.

3 Polish crown with iron until it is dry and shiny, taking care not to burn lighter coloured hoods (fig 3). Mark head line with pins and cut off brim with a craft knife (fig 4). Do not stretch blocked fitting.

4 Take straw brim and shrink central hole until its circumference is slightly less than the head fitting. This is achieved by steaming and pulling central hole edge inward and shrinking away surplus under iron, but take care not to crease it (fig 5). Pre-shape outer brim edge to the approximate brim angle required by using the same method.

5 Pull shrunk brim circle over brim block head fitting. Pin a 1.3cm(½in) grosgrain ribbon around the head fitting, pinning with 'T' pins every 2.5cm(1in) or so (fig 6).

6 Steam and pull brim outwards from centre. Pull evenly along grain, working alternately on one side and then the other, to prevent chasing fullness around the block. Pin outer edge of brim with drawing pins well over the block edge to avoid marking brim surface (fig 7). Polish brim with iron until dry and shiny. Take brim off block.

7 Outer brim can be finished with either a bound edge or a turned edge. For a bound edge wire the brim edge starting at centre back, and bind edge with 1.3cm(½in) grosgrain ribbon (fig 8).

8 For a turned edge, wire brim 1cm(⅜in) inside edge, and turn edge over wire (fig 9). Now press, and then machine along wire impression using a zipper foot. Then either cut raw edge

along machine line or turn in edge again and slip stitch down by hand.

9 To attach crown to brim, match centre back to centre back, and pin crown over brim (fig 10). Join them together using large back stitch, and sew around twice for security. Insert 1.3cm(½in) shaped grosgrain ribbon inside head fitting.

10 Stiffen the straw hat with straw varnish, applied sparingly (fig 11). With straw hats, the stiffener is there to be seen as it imparts a sheen to the surface as well as hardening the straw. Should a hat go limp after wearing, it may be freshened in steam, lightly pressed and then re-stiffened.

Adaptations

The method given above is for a classic style, worked on the most basic, yet one of the most attractive, shapes. Should you have the blocks available, the principles of blocking remain the same for other shapes. Even in the style described, variations can be made. The brim can be turned up at any point, and the crown can be dented in several different ways.

To achieve these variations, gently steam, pull or bend your shape, and hold it in position for a minute or two while it sets. To turn up brims, pull your thumb along the part you are turning up, as if to stretch the straw. Additional help may be got from bending the wire, but only gently or the line will not look natural. Try out these methods on new or old hats, as well as self blocked ones; styles can be changed considerably with only slight variations of line.

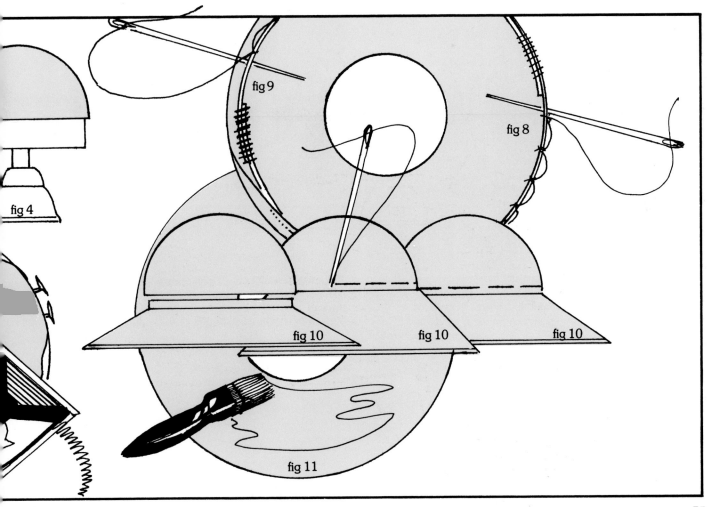

Trimming Straw Hats

If you match a trimming on your straw hat to a detail on your outfit or find a finishing touch that can be used on both your clothes and your hat, you will be able to link your look together and thus enhance its appearance. Thoughtful detailing and considered finishing off do so much for fashion, and by using them carefully fashion looks can be dramatically changed.

Keep the trims you choose neat and witty and avoid overloading, since this will look ridiculous. Such incongruous and precarious creations have helped to give millinery a rather silly image that it certainly does not deserve. Many attractive trims are shown on page 79 but a detailed look at four different trimmings for a Panama straw will show how the fashion character of the basic hat can be changed considerably.

1 A garland of flowers added to a plain straw in high summer is a classic trim idea. Buy a mixture of imitation bunches of flowers, choosing pale toning colours. Break up the bunches and poke the stalks through a head band, building up your own individual mixture and arrangement as you go. Stitch them in place for security. Alternatively you can machine stitch them flat on to a ribbon and then tie the whole string of flowers round the hat in one, although you may need some further in-filling when you see the effect. Try adding grasses and ribbons as well – perfect for a smart summer occassion.

2 For a different and more thought out look, but using the same basic idea, arrange the flowers in a less random way. Group them in one spot, perhaps at the side of the hat, or try four sets evenly distributed for a less formal look. If you use fewer flowers, you will be able to afford better quality ones. Ribbons, grasses, nets, laces or tiny beads can be dropped in behind the bunches of flowers according to taste and this will give the hat an expensive hand-made quality – very different from the single bunch of cherries often encountered hanging limply on many mass produced hats.

3 A Panama straw hat can be sharpened up by adding three or four different braids, but dispense with bows or other additions; the effect will be created by the controlled change of textures. Machine stitch or slip stitch the braids around the head band in contrasting or self colours. It will be marvellous with Chanel type suits or smart summer outfits such as linen blazers and pleated skirts. It will look simple and subtle – a nice understatement.

4 Fabric tied round a straw hat can be linked to part of your clothes. Match the colour to your outfit but perhaps not the pattern. For a very relaxed and casual look try twists of cheesecloth with hitched up long skirts, all ready to play on the beach! Sunglasses obligatory!

More Decorative Trims for Straws

There are a million and one ways to trim a summer straw hat but certain considerations need to be taken into account before you decide on an appropriate decoration. Whether you are using a straw you have blocked yourself or a purchased hat, the choice of trim will be dictated to some extent by the finish between the crown and the brim. Has it been cut or not; is it sewn with a raw edge or has it been neatened and slip stitched together; do the stitch holes show where you have removed a trim from a purchased hat, since unlike felt straw does mark. All these points need to be thought about, for it will be necessary to cover any raw edges and stitch marks with the trim you select. However, as is shown below, this does not mean that you need be restricted in your choice of trim, for there is a wide variety to pick from.

1 A school boy's elasticated snake belt; do Woolworth's still sell them? If you can find one, they are adjustable so will fit any size of head fitting.

2 Any fabric can be frilled up and placed round the hat as a head band. Treat the raw edges with straw stiffener to prevent from fraying, or don't and fringe them deliberately.

3 Make a layered head band of wide grosgrain, medium velvet and narrow satin ribbon. Keep the colours the same and let the textures do all the work.

4 Make a number of fabric rouleaus. Tie several around the crown; stiffen the others and use them to construct a spiky 'flower' which can then be attached to the hat.

5 Sew on to a ribbon flowers, leaves, petals, feathers or anything that is light and flexible. Tie on ribbon and thus the trim – a real flower show finalist!

6 Veiling in pale colours can be sewn around the crown for a really pretty look; use in black under the brim and gathered inside the head fitting for a Mata Hari mystery!

7 String wound round natural straws looks both attractive and unusual. It makes an excellent finish and the range of natural colours, from ecru to hemp, and of textures and thicknesses, is very wide.

8 For 'ultimate technological chic' use a band of plastic or a ring of lightweight metal as a head band. Find a friend who goes to metal work evening classes to prepare one for you! Shiny cardboard which has been cut with raw edges, will have the same type of slick appearance.

9 Rip apart an old hat, stiffen it and from it cut out raw edged shapes. Arrange these on the new hat in whatever pattern you like; you could cluster them in tidy groups or freely scatter all over. Then glue them on.

10 Drape a soft fabric in a turban like technique around the crown as a head band, but remember to cut the fabric on the cross.

11 Braid some ribbons, pressed straw strips, shoelaces or more elaborate items to form a head band – or even mix them all together. Such a band can look smart or pretty, depending on what type of ingredients you use.

12 Gather a 7cm(3in) lace ribbon head band, slot satin ribbon through it and place round hat. Appliqué flowers on to it and scatter some more on the hat itself. If you walk in 5th Avenue, New York on Easter Sunday or in Battersea Park, London on Easter Monday you will be the hit of the Easter Parade.

13 Cut the ends of several types of ribbon into fishtails and use the contrasting self coloured textures as the feature of the decoration on the hat.

14 Most applied decorations, from flowers to stuck on spots, will work just as well under a brim as on top of it. Use a tilted style of hat with a shallow crown so that there is lots of space about the ear and hair line.

15 Straw can be partly coloured or drawn on with inks or fabric paints. Anything goes but do little planned areas rather than all over splashes. It is not difficult but remember that the design will 'bleed' because straw is very absorbent, so it is important to calculate for this in the pattern you decide to use.

16 Studs look fine on straw but only the crown should be treated in this way as the claws will look ugly on the under brim. You can always stud a separate head band so that the hat itself will not be damaged.

17 Since straw is actually made from grasses you can confidently add more. Corn ears, dried flowers and all types of grass will tone beautifully with natural coloured hoods, especially the textured ones like Leghorn.

18 Cut round lace patterns and use these motifs as edge trims on a straw hat. You can also machine round the shapes and cut away the straw beneath, but this is best done when the hat it still in pieces, or on the brim only, if you are using a purchased hat.

19 There are many types of leather straps and belts available, each with a different character. Choose an appropriate strap to go with a particular style of straw hat – smart patent with a tailored straw, Mexican bandit belt with a Western stetson.

20 Designs can be embroidered onto straws by hand or machine. Use embroidery silks in self or contrasting colours and be as adventurous as you like with the designs.

Fashion Looks

Summer straw hats can be as glamorous or as informal as you want to make them. Vary shape, straw type or brim size and they will go with any crisp and cool outfit, whether a stunning silk dress or jeans and a T-shirt.

Cool linen dresses and cotton separates – worn for high summer – at their best with soft and simple straw hats.

Look smart and elegant in sleek tailored straws worn with crisp shirts and sharp collars.

Shady large rough natural straws combined with jeans and cotton vests for sunny days.

Complete an extravagantly frilled high summer look on a special occasion with a decoratively trimmed straw.

Lace Ribbon
Head Band Trim

cut dart around motif

cut dart around motif

fig 6

fig 6

fig 6

fig 3

fig 4

fig 5

overlap darts to curve

fig 1

fig 2

g 7

One of the prettiest trims for a plain straw hat is an appliquéd lace ribbon head band with a butterfly bow finish. Any type of lace ribbon can be used or you can cut a border from a piece of lace, an antique tablecloth or curtain for example, if you have one available. Try threading satin ribbon through lace, or using several different widths of it, or ruching to achieve different, interesting effects.

Materials

A purchased or self-blocked straw hat 1m(1yd) lace ribbon, 3.8cm(1½in) to 6.4cm(2½in) wide. The ribbon illustrated has one decorative edge but it is also available with two.

Method

1 From the lace ribbon cut a head band to head fitting size. Cut ends of band around the motifs so that it will join together exactly when placed around crown (fig 1).

2 Curve lace ribbon head band by making small cuts into it, but follow pattern in the lace when cutting (fig 2). These cuts will be overlapped later and will be invisible in the finished effect.

3 From remaining ribbon cut a centre tie and attach it to headline where head band will join (fig 3). Place head band round crown of hat and arrange, and then pin, overlapped darts to give the necessary curve.

4 Pin meeting point of head band and squeeze ends together into a soft fold. Stab stitch down to straw (fig 4). Now stab stitch head band to hat all round, including the overlapped darts (fig 5). Add a few more stitches to bottom edge of ribbon at headline to prevent it riding up.

5 Prepare a lace bow from rest of ribbon in the form of a butterfly of two pairs of motifs. Cut out butterfly shapes and place one over the other, at different angles. Squeeze together and oversew (fig 6).

6 Place bow on hat at head band meeting point, pin, and then sew, in position. Roll centre tie over bow centre and tuck under. Firmly but invisibly stab stitch centre tie, bow and ribbon meeting point in one (fig 7).

Cut out wide lace for a more irregular trim.

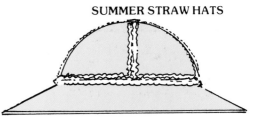

Decorate crown of hat at quarterly intervals with a fine lace ribbon to match the head band.

Gather large lace motifs at their centres for a head band with more of a three dimensional effect.

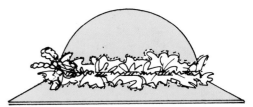

Place lace ribbon, gathered with a double row of large stitches, around crown, and cover ends with extra motif.

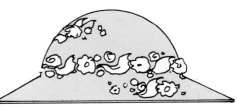

Appliqué motifs cut from lace ribbon on to both crown and brim to link up with head band.

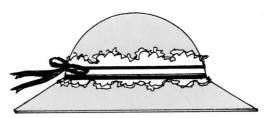

Add plain ribbon over lace head band.

Wound Ribbon Trim

fig 1

fig 2

fig 3

fig 4

fig 5

fig 6

fig 7

A ribbon wound round the crown of a simple straw hat at interesting angles is a really original and different type of trim. Satin ribbon in different colors will look super and grosgrain ribbon strung with flowers spectacular. Use furnishing braids and glittery or metallic ribbon for an even more eye-catching effect. Whatever you choose, remember to arrange and wind the ribbon on the hat while it is on the block. Then steam well to set the trimming, otherwise the accumulated tension produced by wrapping the ribbon round and round the crown will make the straw buckle.

Materials
A purchased or self-blocked straw hat
Up to 3m(3yd) ribbon, 0.6cm(¼in) wide, or any other suitable strip decoration

Method
1 Curve the ribbon under the iron as it will then sit better on the crown (fig 1).

2 Attach one end of ribbon at centre back of hat about 1.3cm(½in) up from headline (fig 2). Stab stitch in position; this start will be covered by first winding of ribbon (fig 3).

3 Wind the ribbon round the crown at interesting random angles and pin at intervals to control it (fig 4). Try not to hide one layer with another.

4 Tuck under final end at the side you plan to place the finishing detail (fig 5). Trim end flush with ribbon it is tucked under (fig 6). Stab stitch end just under covering ribbon with as few stitches as possible.

5 Stab stitch some of the windings to the hat for security, always working beneath the covering ribbon.

6 Prepare a bow with fishtail ends and sew onto disguised ribbon end, and stab stitch in place invisibly (fig 7).

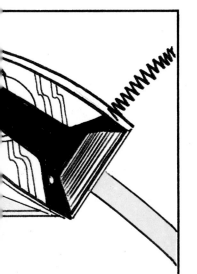

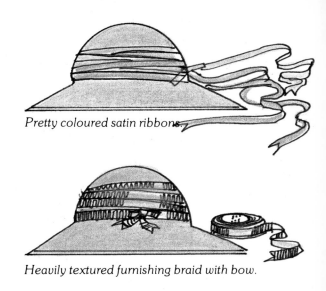

Pretty coloured satin ribbons.

Heavily textured furnishing braid with bow.

Lace ribbon and appliquéd lace motif.

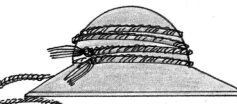

Silk cord with matching tassels.

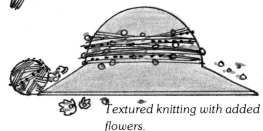

Textured knitting with added flowers.

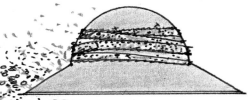

Metallic braid with a tinsel finish.

Embroidered ribbon.

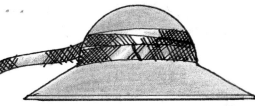

Moiré ribbon for a glossy sheen.

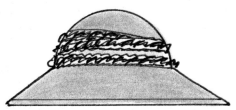

Twisted ribbon for a three-dimensional effect.

Decorative Flower Trim

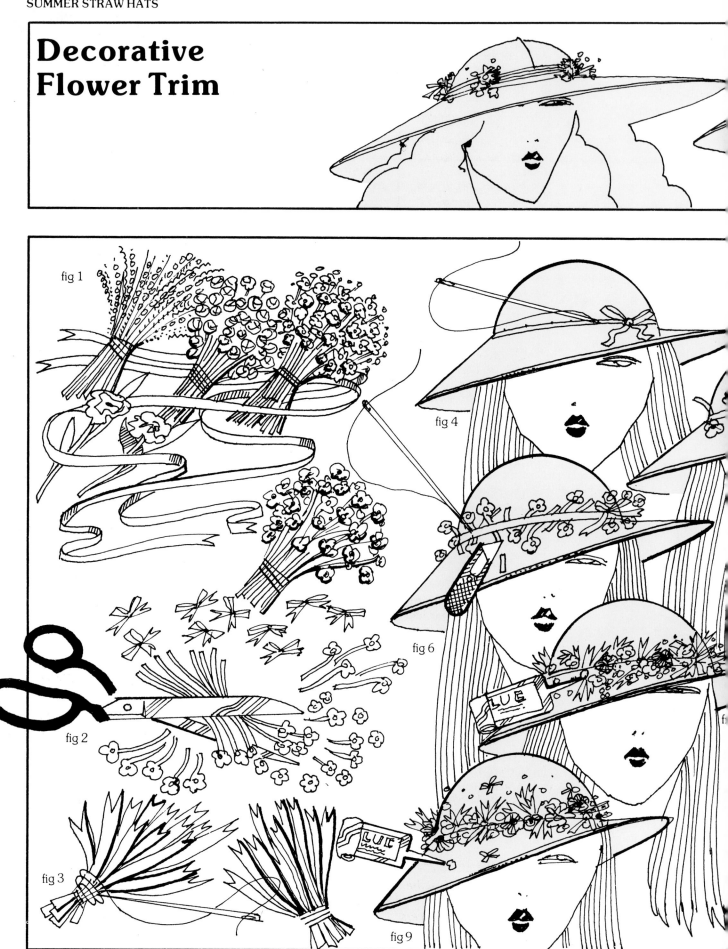

fig 1

fig 4

fig 6

fig 2

fig 3

fig 9

Nothing will look more appropriate on a hot summer's day than a shady straw hat trimmed with seasonal flowers and ribbons. As is shown here, you can mix all sorts of imitation flowers together, or just use several large blooms. Keep both ribbons and flowers toned for a subtle effect, rather than using contrasting gaudy colours. And whatever arrangement of flowers you choose, do not overload it; the effect should be interesting and attractive, but the trim should not be out of balance with the hat by the time it is finished.

Materials

A purchased or self-blocked straw hat
About a dozen bunches of small mixed imitation flowers including: verbena, lily of the valley, rosebuds, mixed posies, stamens and leaves (fig 1)
3m(3yd) satin ribbon

Method

1 Cut the fine wire around stems of flower bunches. Trim off flower stalks to different lengths, taking stalks right off some flowers, so that the result is as varied as possible (fig 2).

2 Cut 61cm(24in) from the ribbon for the head band. Cut remainder of ribbon into 5.1cm(2in) oblique cut lengths. From these lengths bind groups together in threes and fours, and also make some tiny bows (fig 3).

3 Tie head band ribbon round crown along the headline (fig 4) and stab stitch it to hat for security every 4cm(1½in).

4 Arrange flowers all around hat, inserting stems from above and below ribbon (fig 5). Tack stems along headline to hat as you proceed, stitching from the back (fig 6); trim off stems that protrude too much.

5 Attach bunches of ribbons to the head band, stab stitching them through as you go (fig 7). Over all gaps, visible stitches, meeting points, ribbon middles or raw edges, glue flower heads without stems (fig 8).

6 Final touches can now be added. Stitch down tiny bows, or glue directly on to hat tiny flowers, leaves and stamens to complete decoration (fig 9).

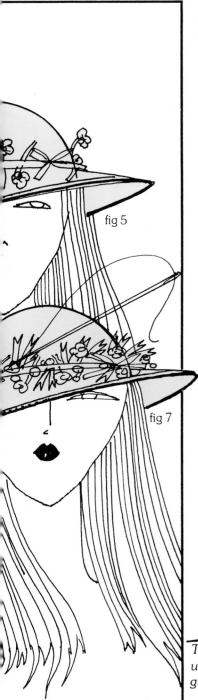

fig 5

fig 7

Try flowers against the underbrim, either groups or single flowers.

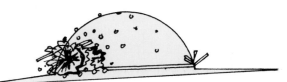

Arrange flowers in four bunches. Add a ribbon head band and place bunches on it at regular intervals.

Make up a special bunch of large and small flowers. Place on head band and stick flower heads onto brim and crown.

Stick small flowers all over hat and spike with larger flower heads and leaves which should be sewn on.

Sew flowers on to a loose ribbon long enough to tie around crown with a knot or bow.

Try colouring with inks or dyes the areas behind the flowers to create a shadowy effect.

Use single dramatic flowers or pairs such as roses or camellias.

Knitted Hats

Knit fabrics are particularly suitable for the millinery beginner to work with, as their stretching property means that the fit does not have to be absolutely accurate. Styling of knitted hats is usually simple, with changes of fashion being reflected more in choice of colour, yarn and stitch than in basic shapes. For these reasons, and its warmth and casualness, the knitted hat has become a classic.

Knitted fabric is soft and pliable and will hug the head, so hat shapes should take advantage of this. Many simple stitches are suitable for hats, but bear in mind that the main part of the crown should be in quite a firm stitch, while the edging or turnback should be in a springy elastic stitch such as rib, so that the hat will cling to the head. If you want to create a hat that has a more definite shape, use crochet rather than knitting, as this gives a fabric with more body. With a firm yarn and a dense stitch, such as single or double crochet, quite complicated shapes can be developed, such as pillboxes, forage caps and small brim styles.

One of the advantages of hand knitting or crocheting a hat is that all the shaping can be done as the fabric is created, so that hardly any sewing will remain to be done. For this reason it is preferable when knitting to use four double-ended needles to avoid having a centre back seam. Any make of knitting machine can also be used to make hats. It is simpler to make the hat in separate sections on the machine, and then sew them together, as it will be difficult to shape the hat integrally on the machine. However, you can take advantage of the techniques of the machine to make a hat quickly in an interesting textured pattern or a complicated multi-coloured Fair Isle design, which would take hours on hand needles.

Experiment with making knitted or crocheted trims for your hats. Knitted rouleaus or chunky crocheted chain can be threaded through hats, wound round them, or braided into a trim. Woolly pompons need not be restricted to ski-caps; several small ones would make a lively trim on any shape. Tassels and crochet buttons are easy to make and can be used in lots of different ways. Match up knitted hats and trims to sweaters, scarves, gloves, mittens and even socks for warm co-ordinated winter looks.

Knitting Yarns and Stitches

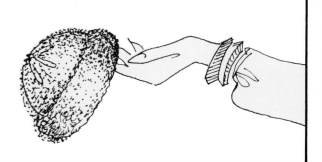

Yarns

Knitted hats can be made out of a wide variety of different yarns. Use any wool, acrylic or blended yarns in thicknesses from 4 ply to double-double knit for winter styles; the same shapes can easily be turned into cool summery hats by making them in cotton or linen mixture yarns. The guidelines given here to the choice of appropriate yarns refer intentionally to examples made mostly by Pingouin and Paton since these are available internationally, but any similar types of yarn from other manufacturers can of course be used.

A smooth plain yarn will show up textured stitches to their best advantage. Pingouin's 'Super 4', 'Sport' and 'Iceberg' and Paton's 'Beehive' and 'Capstan' come in a wide range of colours. A tweedy look can be achieved by using mixture or marled yarns. Mixture yarns are made by mixing together yarn fibres of different colours before the spinning process to give a gently mottled effect. Marled yarns consist of two or more fine yarns of different colours twisted to make a speckled fabric. These techniques create such yarns as Pingouin's 'La Houle' and 'Tweedé', and Paton's 'Bracken Tweed'.

Take advantage of the new and interesting textured yarns such as boucles, which are spun so that loops project from the yarn, and unevenly spun knopped and slubbed yarns. Pingouin's 'Cythère' and 'Tumulte' create very individual surfaces; try striping them with co-ordinating smooth yarns to achieve an exciting, textured fabric even from plain knitting.

For a deliciously soft and flattering hat, try an angora or mohair mixture; for a knit fabric that looks and feels like velvet, try chenille which is made from two strong fine yarns twisted tightly round thousands of soft short pile fibres. It is at its best used for a head-hugging cap or a floppy beret for evening wear.

Rayon yarns, such as J. Henry Smith's 'Pearl' or 'Ideal', will also produce fashionable evening hats with a silky sheen, and they can also be used to make fringe and tassel trims for all kinds of hats. Many lurex yarns, including Pingouin's 'Place Vendôme' and J. Henry Smith's 'Silverknit', are available. Use them in narrow strips to liven up plainer yarns or for tiny glittering beanies.

Remember that knitted hats are not just suitable for winter wear. The air pockets in knitting which give warmth in winter will also keep you cool in summer. Use cotton or linen mixture yarns or unusually textured ones, such as Pingouin's 'Eaux Vives' and 'Coton Rustique', and Paton's 'Jacana'. Firm cotton yarns like Pingouin's 'Coton Naturel' and Coat's 'Mercer Crochet' can be crocheted into a hat with a small shady brim. For a beach hat use fine twine or raffia, either real or synthetic (such as Nottingham Handcrafts' 'Raffene'). Crochet it with a big floppy brim, or just make a brim only and wear it over a brightly coloured headscarf.

Stitches

The following knitting and crochet stitches can all be used for making attractive and practical knitted hats such as those shown on the following pages.

Rib Stitch The basic standby stitch for making knitted hats. Use it in all varieties from 1×1 to bold 4×4. For a hat with a deep turnback, knit the crown in 1×1 to give a small head shape, but change to 3×3 for the chunky turnback.

Cable Stitch Cable stitches make decorative knitted hats, but they restrict the stretch of the fabric, so it is best to combine them with rib stitches to keep the fabric elastic.

Stocking (Stockinette) Stitch Use this stitch for fancy yarns or stripes, or combine with a more decorative stitch on the turnback of the hat.

Textured Stitches Moss stitch, basketweave stitch and honeycomb stitch are all ideal for hats, as are all the classic Aran stitches.

Lace Stitches These can be used for small pull-on hats, but are not really very suitable for adults' hats, as the fabric produced will be too floppy.

Fair Isle Stitches These can make wonderful hats, rich with colour and pattern. Remember that the floats at the back will restrict the stretching property of the fabric, so ensure that the hat will be big enough.

Chevron Stitches Use these to give zig-zag edges to all types of knitted hats.

Welted Fabric Several rows of stocking (stockinette) stitch followed by several rows of reverse stocking (stockinette) stitch will give a dramatic edge to a hat when the rest of the crown is in plain knitted fabric. Welting increases fabric width, so when changing to plain fabric, increase 1 stitch in every 6 to counteract this effect.

Crochet Stitches Use single or double crochet to make a firm fabric. Treble crochet, and variations of it, are suitable for a soft crown, as are plain shell stitch or basket stitch. For a firmer crown use daisy stitch, leaf stitch or forget-me-not stitch. For an interesting turnback use bobble stitch, which can also be used to make a bobble pattern over a double crochet crown. For a fake fur look on a warm winter hat use loop stitches.

Knitted Hat Types

Knitted hats can be just as versatile as other hat types; as is shown here there is a mass of original shapes and styles to choose from. Make them up in interestingly coloured and textured yarns and match them to scarves, gloves, mittens, or sweaters to complete the effect.

1 The simplest tiny beany hat can be knitted or crocheted in a firm moss stitch or single crochet. Make it with integral shaping or in separate sections. It is a perfect excuse for knitting a complicated and interesting design.

2 A beany made in luxurious yarn, such as rayon, chenille or lurex, is ideal as an evening hat. For an effective zig-zag edging use a chevron stitch in striped colours.

3 Balaclavas can be very practical. Use a plain stitch, with a ribbed neck and edges to keep the shape, in a soft yarn. Add a peak to turn it into a functional skiing helmet, remembering to sandwich a firm interlining between the two peak sections.

4 A warm scarf-hat can be made by folding a long knitted scarf in half and stitching down one side of it for about 15cm (6in) from the fold.

5 For effective brimmed knitted cloches use a crochet stitch in a smooth wool crêpe yarn such as Pingouin's 'Papotages'.

6 Try out different brim shapes in firm yarns and single or double crochet stitches.

7 For shady beach hats use cotton yarn, twine or raffia; larger brims will always be floppy when knitted or crocheted.

8 Winter sports hats will work best in smooth wool yarns with rib edges to grip the head tightly. Trim with wool pompons or tassels.

9 Norwegian and Fair Isle patterns are perfect for ski-caps, the proper accessory for classically fashionable ski sweaters.

10 Match up a scarf, gloves or sweater to a knitted hat in an Aran stitch in plain or coloured wools. Oiled wool will make it waterproof, but it will be wonderfully warm anyway.

11 A knitted beret shape can be adapted in lots of ways. A big floppy one in tartan colours will look good with a kilt; a smaller one is less casual, more elegant. Experiment with looser textured stitches, or try bouclé or chenille yarns.

12 To achieve a fun-fur effect, which is particulary suitable for berets, use loop stitches in hand knitting or pile machine-knitting.

13 For an effective pill-box hat use a firm crochet stitch.

14 The simplest roll-up hat can be made in many ways. Double or treble crochet are both suitable, as are plain or fine rib knitting; try them in soft yarns such as angora or mohair.

15 A very plain silky roll-up knitted hat with a tiny turnback will look simple but sophisticated.

16 To give a roll-up hat a warmer feel use a deeper turnback. Experiment with different stitches – a fine all-over stitch for the crown and something more dramatic and chunky, like cables or heavy twisted ribs, for the turnback.

Roll-Up Knitted Hat

This roll-up knitted hat is made in stocking (stockinette) stitch from a classic basic pattern, and it is integrally shaped, avoiding the need to make it in sections, which then have to be sewn together. Vary the basic style by making it in different yarns, in brightly coloured stripes, or with a fluffy turnback, but do not change the stitch. Since it is a reversible hat, you can wear it with a smooth crown and a textured turnback or vice versa.

Materials
3 balls Pingouin's 'Laine et Angora' or
2 balls Pingouin's 'Type Shetland'
4 double ended needles, size 4mm (USA No 5)

Method
1 Knit a tension swatch before starting. The required stitch size should give 30 rows and 24 stitches to 10cm(4in). If necessary use larger or smaller needles to give correct stitch size.

2 Cast on 120 stitches, and working in circular knitting, knit 10 rows in purl stitch. Then:
Row 10: Change to plain knitting; knit 34 rows
Row 44: Dec 1 st every 10th st for 1 row. Knit 4 rows
Row 49: Dec 1 st every 9th st for 1 row. Knit 4 rows
Row 54: Dec 1 st every 8th st for 1 row. Knit 2 rows
Row 57: Dec 1 st every 7th st for 1 row. Knit 1 row
Row 59: Dec 1 st every 6th st for 1 row. Knit 1 row
Row 61: Dec 1 st every 5th st for 1 row. Knit 1 row
Row 63: Knit 2 together to end.

3 Break yarn and thread through stitches. Draw up tightly, and fasten off on smooth side of knitting.

4 If you want a deeper turnback than that given above, cast on 120 stitches and work in knit 3, purl 3 rib for 12cm(4¾in), then change to plain knitting and continue as above from row 10 on.

Seven Section Beret

This knitted beret in seven sections can be made either by hand or on a knitting machine. Follow the arrangement of the colours on the graph, using the colour scheme suggested here, or choosing your own. If you are planning to make it on a machine, try out the Fair Isle variation and match it to a Fair Isle sweater or gloves.

Materials
1 ball Pingouin's 'Laine et Mohair/Amiral 01' (Colour A)
1 ball Pingouin's 'Laine et Mohair/Plomb 42' (Colour B)
1 ball Pingouin's 'Laine et Mohair/Bourgogne 38' (Colour C)
1 ball Pingouin's 'Laine et Mohair/Colvert 32' (Colour D)
1 pair needles, size 3mm (USA No 2) and
1 pair needles, size 3.75mm (USA No 4) or:
Any knitting machine

Method for Hand Knitting
1 Knit a tension swatch before starting on hat. The required stitch size should give 30 rows and 22 stitches to 10cm(4in) on size 3.75mm (USA No 4) needles. Use larger or smaller needles if necessary to give correct stitch size.

2 Following graph for striping sequence of colours, knit each of the seven sections as follows. Cast on 16 stitches on size 3mm (USA No 2) needles. Knit in 1 knit, 1 purl rib for 8 rows.

3 At row 8, change to size 3.75mm (USA No 4) needles and stocking (stockinette) stitch. Increase 1 stitch each side of this row, and every 3rd row for 16 rows (to give 28 stitches); then knit 2 rows straight. At row 26, decrease 1 stitch each side of every 4th row for 48 rows.

4 Break yarn at row 74, thread it through remaining 4 stitches, draw up and fasten off.

5 Steam press each of seven sections now made, except for the ribs. Then using the yarn in the main colour, join sections together in back stitch, matching them row for row. For a really professional finish, place hat on dolly and steam again, but not the rib.

Method for Machine Knitting
1 Knit a tension swatch to determine correct setting for stocking (stockinette) stitch and suitable tension for rib. Then, if you have a rib machine, knit beret following instructions for hand knitting, starting at step 2.

2 If you do not have a rib machine, cast on 14 stitches and knit 18 rows on a stitch setting one whole number tighter than the main fabric setting. At row 18, pick up cast-on row to form a hem. Increase one stitch each side, loosen stitch setting to main fabric tension, turn row counter back to 8. Then continue as above, starting at row 8 (step 3).

Striped Beret   *Fair Isle Beret*

☐ *colour A*   ◩ *colour B*   ⊠ *colour C*   ⊙ *colour D*

Pattern Adaptation

For a Fair Isle beret use size 4mm (USA No 5) needles for main fabric, or slightly looser machine setting. Following the Fair Isle chart, knit as above. The chart can be transferred to any 24 stitch repeat punchcard for machine knitting. Work in the centre of the machine bed so that the design is properly centralized. Use the following colours or choose your own:

1 ball Pingouin's 'Type Shetland/Beige 23' (Colour A)
1 ball Pingouin's 'Type Shetland/Gris Moyen 14' (Colour B)
1 ball Pingouin's 'Type Shetland/Faience 22' (Colour C)
1 ball Pingouin's 'Type Shetland/Paprika 09' (Colour D)

Bridal Headdresses

A traditional style of dress is still often required for formal weddings, and for these occasions the outfit of the bride needs to be appropriate for the holy ceremony and yet as glamorous and attractive as she wants. The function of the bridal veil to cover the head and face is also traditional, but it has to serve a decorative purpose as well. It must complement the grand long dress, the satins, silks and ruffles, the train and bouquet it is to be teamed with, and at the same time keep the hair and head interesting and special.

Bridal headdresses are mostly worn with veils of one type or another, and the shape of the veil will dictate the size and choice of decoration to be added. Depending on the type of veil you choose, large single flowers, tiny bunches, or deep heavier circlets can all be suitable. Instructions are given in this chapter for making several different styles of veil and for several types of decoration as well as lots of ideas for interesting bridal headdress looks.

The techniques involved in making up the headdresses and veils are quite simple and a minimum of sewing is required. Flowers can be bound together with wire or sewing thread and trims can be similarly attached to their bases. It is only the final veil attachment where discreet secure stitching is necessary, but this can also be kept to a minimum, since all the materials to be used will be light and easy to work with.

As well as showing some of the classical ways of making a bridal headdress as pretty and alluring as befits the occasion without being too overloaded, this chapter looks at some alternative types of bridal headwear. If you do not want to adhere strictly to tradition, there are many other kinds of headdress which still retain the elements of covering the head in a decorative though more unusual way, to choose from. If a half veil and a glittering tiara are not your style, you will find some interesting alternatives, including brimmed hats and lacy headscarves.

Unlike most hats, the bridal headdress is created almost totally for its decorative effect. Beautiful and delicate detail allied to simple and effective shapes will give a sense of style in real fashion terms. Remember that you will be looking at the photographs for the next fifty years, so the headdress must be right!

Ideas for Bridal Headdresses

A whole gallery of bridal headdress styles can be created, ranging from the very traditional to the more formal, despite the limited but appropriate colour schemes usually used. Of the ideas for headdresses given here, not all have long veils, and many are without face veils. If you like the idea of a face veil, you can pin it to the front decoration, or try a multi-layered veil, the top part of which can be pulled forward over the face. Remember that if you do choose a headdress with a veil, it is well worth finishing off the veil properly. Most ready-made versions come with raw edges, but they look so much better with either a satin ribbon edging or perhaps an added lace border. All the extra effort will be repaid by a really professional end result.

You may want to take your veil off at the reception. If this is the case, either make the veil detachable from its fitting device, if you want to continue to wear the decorative part, or prepare an additional decoration to put in the hair instead to retain the illusion. On all bridal headdresses the fitting is very important. Veiling is so light that you can use a mass of it in any length but you will want to feel that it is totally secure. All sorts of different fittings can be used to keep the veil in place: circlets, sprung wires, Alice bands and bobby pins or grips. Combs can also make good bases for decorations if your hair is not too fine.

1 Attach ribbons of any length to the sides of a simple circlet. For an even more decorative look sew tiny flowers all down the ribbons; the idea can be repeated in your bouquet.

2 Place groups of flowers over each ear and gather all the veiling into these points.

3 An antique lace table-cloth, a christening mantle or family heirloom will look beautiful without any other added features; attach it to the simplest circlet.

4 Use the same kind of lace but hold it in place with lace flowers. If you make the flowers from new lace, tint it (by dipping in tea) to match the old.

5 If you have any dress material, such as silk or chiffon, left over, use it to make petals and leaves. Stiffen the fabric before cutting with a mixture of equal parts of straw stiffener and clear methylated spirits. Combine the petals with some lace flowers and add to a lace edged veil.

6 Pleated chiffon or silk made into an elaborate back of hair decoration looks good from all sides. Wear it with a 1920s type veil, pulled into the back of the neck rather like a giant scarf.

7 To liven up miles of plain veiling, appliqué beads, lace motifs or tiny flowers all over it.

8 Using the same kind of appliqué, place the motifs you chose in strategic clusters on the veil, rather than at random.

9 Wear a skull cap chicly to one side. Attach a veil two-thirds of the way round it, and hide the gathers with flowers and ribbons.

10 Try using a mass of millinery veiling. It is rather narrow, but dotted cotton net is wider and softer, and used in quantity, looks splendid.

11 Drape and secure the veil at one side if the design of the wedding dress permits it.

12 Simple waxy camellias, very sculptured, very Garbo, are best with dark, elegant hair.

13 White goose feathers are the bridal equivalent of the 1950s feathered half-hat and can be bought ready mounted onto leno pads.

14 Make a satin ribbon snood and decorate it with interwoven fresh or imitation flowers.

Flower Circlet Headdress

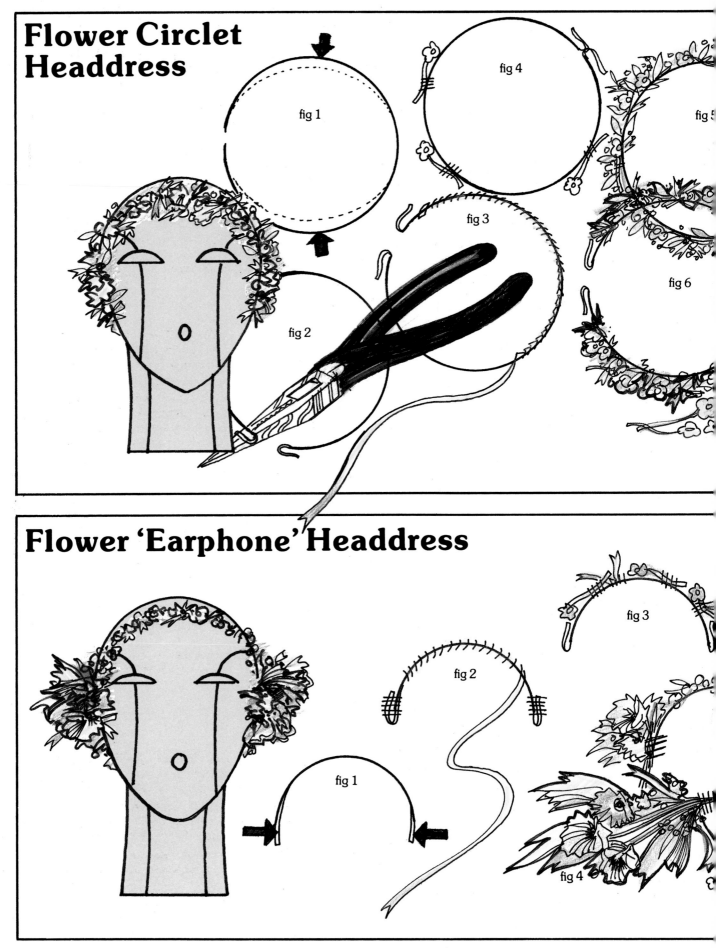

fig 1

fig 2

fig 3

fig 4

fig 5

fig 6

Flower 'Earphone' Headdress

fig 1

fig 2

fig 3

fig 4

This pretty circlet can be worn with a veil or on its own. Make it with your own self-made flowers (see page 110) or with fresh flowers. Choose several types of species in white and creams and tints of other pale colours; avoid dead white as it looks very flat. You can even deliver a prepared wire to your florist so that the circlet and bouquet can be co-ordinated.

Materials
Heavy gauge millinery wire, cut to head measurement plus 5cm(2in) for fastening loops. Average length is 61cm(24½in)
Wedding dress material, cut on the cross,
either: long enough to yield strips to wind round wire,
or: long enough to sew lengthways along wire
7 bunches of small artificial flowers
1m(1yd) baby satin ribbon in white, cream or similar tints

Method
1 Make a head fitting by bending the millinery wire into an oval shape (fig 1). With pliers bend hooks at either end of wire fitting so that they will hook into one another without twisting the oval (fig 2). These hooks are the centre back of circlet.

2 Wind the strips of fabric round and round wire or cover it by oversewing fabric on it lengthwise (fig 3).

3 Break down bunches of flowers (see page 87) and start adding them evenly to circlet by wrapping thread over individual stems (fig 4). Remember all decoration must run along outwards from wire to leave head fitting clean inside.

4 Continue to add flowers, taking first one type, then another and so on. Add any leaves or ribbons by oversewing onto head fitting (fig 5). Fill in gaps, cover visible stitches and disguise stitches on ribbon centres with flower heads. Glue on singly or in groups but leave hooks clear (fig 6).

5 Hook circlet together on the head to check fit; if it is not perfect, adjust hooks accordingly. Wear with a veil or on its own (fig 7).

Another attractive bridal headdress that also features flowers as its main decoration is this 'earphone' style. In this case the decorated wire is placed over the head from ear to ear rather than around it, the flowery earphones forming the focal points.

Materials
Heavy gauge millinery wire, cut long enough to reach from ear to ear plus 10cm(4in) for fastening loops
Strip of wedding dress material cut on the cross, long enough to wind around wire
5 mixed bunches of tiny artificial flowers
4 larger artificial flowers such as roses or carnations
1m(1yd) satin ribbon
1m(1yd) velvet ribbon
Reel of fine wire

Method
1 Out of millinery wire make a sprung half circle to grip the head from ear to ear (fig 1). Turn back ends of half circle with pliers and bind with thread to form loops. Wind fabric round and round wire to cover it (fig 2).

2 Break down bunches of flowers and prepare ribbons into bunches or bows (see page 87). Start adding flowers and ribbons to wire by wrapping thread over stems and ends, leaving loops free to take larger flowers (fig 3).

3 Make up two matching bunches of flowers, using the larger roses or carnations, spiked with tiny flowers and ribbons. Bind them tightly together with fine wire (fig 4).

4 Sew bunches to loops on either side of head wire, making sure that loops are totally covered (fig 5). Fill in any gaps or untidy ends by glueing on extra flower heads (fig 6).

Traditional Veils on Circlets

fig 1

fig 2

fig 3

fig 5

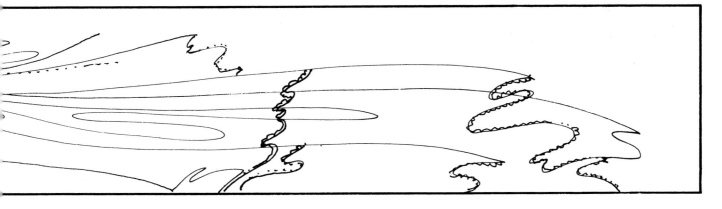

fig 6

fig 7

Here are three traditional wedding veils that might be worn with the flower circlet just described, or with other plain or differently decorated circlets. All three may be used singly or with two or more layers for a more extravagant appearance; if you go for a layered look, shape each layer separately. Silk veiling is available in both 182cm(72in) and 274cm (108in) widths, so there should be no need to join it – unless of course you wish to fill the nave of Westminster Abbey with your train! It is quite acceptable to leave the veiling edges raw but finishing them off with lace or satin ribbon does produce a much better effect. Remember to add these finishes before you gather the veiling.

A Full Veil For this look use a covered untrimmed circlet and a full width of silk veiling as long as you require; for a double veil, you will need double the chosen length. Gather veiling evenly across width, with two rows of large machine stitching (fig 1), to three-quarters of the measurement of the circlet. Fold edge of gathered veil over circlet, and oversew to inside, first in one direction and then in the other to form a firm criss cross stitch (fig 2). Cut veil edges to desired length and shape (fig 3). Hang up to avoid creasing. If double veiling is required, shape the under veil before gathering.

A Layered Veil For this look use a covered untrimmed circlet, a full veil of 182cm(72in) width, and four graduating semicircles of veiling; each should be smaller than the previous one, the smallest forming the face veil (fig 4). Cut long veil to shape and gather as described above. Gather each smaller veil at the centre, reducing by a third to half the measurement of the circlet. Pin circlet and veils together to gauge effect when placed on the head. Adjust if necessary. Turn veiling in over circlet and oversew to inside with firm criss cross stitches. Adjust individual veil shapes at bottom if necessary. Add decorations to circlet.

A Circular Veil For this look use a covered untrimmed circlet, 3m(3yd) veiling 274cm(108in) wide for a single layer or 6m(6yd) for a double look. Cut a complete circle from the veiling of 274cm(108in) diameter. Place circle over head and allow to cascade around(fig 5). Arrange it to suit your requirements – equal length all round or short front, long train, and so on. Place circlet over head and mark its line on the veiling with tacking stitches (fig 6). Remove circlet and gather veiling evenly by hand along the tacking line, arranging gathering as you want, making it fuller at the back or sides (fig 7). Attach veil to inside of circlet with criss cross stitching. If desired trim veiling front or back to any length required. Add decorations to circlet.

Fashion Look

To create a total bridal look match up the colouring and textures of dress and veiling or use the same fabric for both. Co-ordinate the colours used in flower circlets with other ribbon and flower trims for the best effect.

Less Traditional Bridal Ideas

Many people still like the idea of a bride wearing some kind of head covering, but this does not mean that it is essential to choose a full length veil. There are all sorts of attractive and less traditional alternatives, so pick one that goes well with your dress, is appropriate to the style of the wedding, and that you feel happy wearing.

Try wearing an interesting novelty straw hat with a white texture in the weave and sprinkled with flowers and white beads. Add some millinery veiling, gathered and caught beneath the head band. It can be decorated with white confetti: horseshoes, dots and hearts. Put these on with touches of glue where the veil strands cross. You will retain the wedding day feeling but look interestingly different.

To a circular base decorated with white or cream silky braids add two huge bunches of natural grasses and dried flowers. Leave some natural but spray others with white cellulose paint. They will be glossy and sculptured and very striking. Give them several days to dry so that no trace of a paint smell is left.

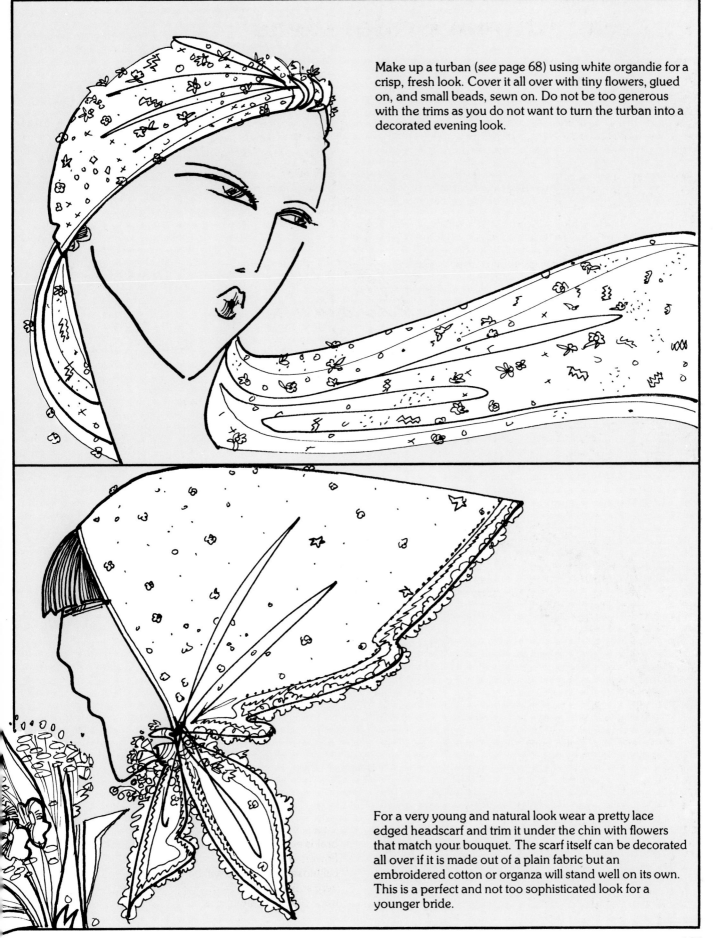

Make up a turban (*see* page 68) using white organdie for a crisp, fresh look. Cover it all over with tiny flowers, glued on, and small beads, sewn on. Do not be too generous with the trims as you do not want to turn the turban into a decorated evening look.

For a very young and natural look wear a pretty lace edged headscarf and trim it under the chin with flowers that match your bouquet. The scarf itself can be decorated all over if it is made out of a plain fabric but an embroidered cotton or organza will stand well on its own. This is a perfect and not too sophisticated look for a younger bride.

Hair Decorations

There are bound to be some occasions when a hat will not seem appropriate, and there are likely to be some outfits with which a hat will not look absolutely right. In these cases a headdress or hair decoration is more often than not the answer. Headdresses are not just the property of the bride or the leading lady; they can be as simple and casual, or as extravagant and formal as you like, but will complete and complement perfectly any fashion look, from jeans to an elegant evening dress. They can be worn at any time of day and at any season of the year if you choose suitable trims. Try a simple flowered clip by day, a glossy, sophisticated comb decoration by night. Complete young summer outfits with head bands, ribbons, or coloured combs; sleek winter day looks with feather or leather trimmed decorations.

Though hair decorations may take many forms, and can be decorated in an overwhelming range of ways, styles are limited to those that can be attached comfortably to the head; lightness and security are also of prime importance. Both head bands and Alice or sprung half bands can be used successfully, but the neatest and most secure way to attach a decoration firmly in the hair is to use either grips (bobby pins) or combs. Of these, the comb is not only the most convenient to use, but it also forms the best base on which to build the decoration. Most trims such as feathers and flowers can easily be wired or sewn round the comb between its teeth, while sequins, small bows and braids can be glued to its top edge.

Practically any type of trim can be mounted on to combs, and the variety of different looks that can be achieved is therefore endless. For light, pretty looks add small satin bows and ribbons, lace motifs or small flowers. For later day looks try velvet ribbons, sequins, feathers, lamé braids, pleated fabric, or jewellery – fake or real. For country, sporty looks experiment with leather, yarns, even fishing flies.

Flowers suit all occasions, but choose the species carefully. Use fresh flowers if you think they will last, or some of the beautiful imitation ones available. Most department stores have an artificial flower counter and the range they offer is enormous – as vast as nature itself. The best examples from France are quite expensive, but as is described on the next page, it is comparatively simple to make your own, which can often look just as effective. Choose fresh spring flowers, such as daisies, buttercups and cornflowers for easy cotton looks; mixed posies, roses and blossoms for high summer; and camellias or orchids in strong colours or natural tints for special occasions and evenings.

Flower Making and Flower Headdresses

Although making very exotic and highly realistic artificial flowers is a skilled and complicated business, it is possible to produce beautiful imitation flowers at home using an iron and some straw stiffener. Try this pretty rose on a stem for a start; you can easily change the flower type by cutting differently shaped petals, but the basic construction principles will remain the same. Once you have made one or two you will feel more ambitious, and can start creating whole floral decorations from flowers, stems, leaves and even nets and pleated fabrics, to produce quite elaborate flower headdresses, such as those shown here.

Materials

½m(½yd) fabric or fabric pieces. Start with simple cottons with body. Avoid very loosely woven fabrics, and very fine ones which are hard to handle. Tweeds and leathers can be uses successfully.
20.5cm(8in) millinery wire

Method

1 First stiffen your chosen fabric to give it body, to help in the shaping process, and to prevent it fraying, since the edges are left raw. Paint on the stiffening mixture of half straw stiffener and half clear methylated spirits for fine and medium fabrics, and neat straw stiffener for heavier types. Allow half an hour for it to dry.

2 From the stiffened fabric cut on the cross a series of strips from 2cm(¾in) to 7.5cm(3in) wide. Cut one longer narrow strip for the stem (fig 1).

3 Fold strips over and over into squares (fig 2). Prepare petal pattern templates in card (fig 3). Place templates on folded fabric and cut out petal shapes on the cross, several at a time (fig 4).

4 Pull individual petals into desired shapes on tip of a hot iron; the heat will melt stiffener which will then immediately re-set into the new petal shapes (fig 5).

5 Prepare stem from the millinery wire, making a small loop at the top end. Make the flower centre by folding a 5cm(2in) square piece of fabric over twice, and wrapping it over and around the looped wire end (fig 6).

6 Start adding petals one by one round and round the flower centre, wrapping them on very tightly with thread and adding the occasional stitch. Make sure centre feels packed tight and not at all loose in the fingers. Always wind petals on in the same place and avoid letting the thread ride down the stem (fig 7). Continue until all petals have been added; leaves, buds or other additional features can now be attached in the same way, if required (fig 8).

7 When flower head is complete, roll out edges of outer petals over a hot needle to imitate a blown rose (fig 9).

8 Complete stem by wrapping thin crossway strip of fabric tightly round and round it, neatening petal bottoms and stitches at flower end (fig 10). Secure at both ends by stitching or glueing for a neat finish.

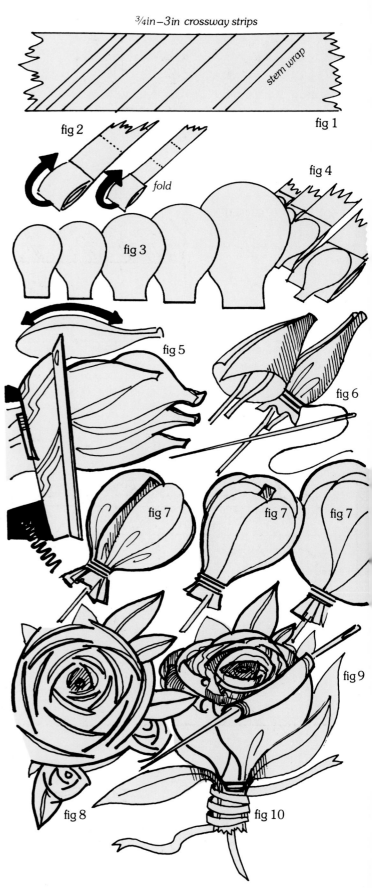

¾in–3in crossway strips

stem wrap

fig 1

fig 2

fold

fig 3

fig 4

fig 5

fig 6

fig 7

fig 7

fig 7

fig 8

fig 9

fig 10

1 Flowered headdress to match neckband.

2 Flowery ribbons from a headdress.

3 Flowers on an Alice band.

4 Flowers with pompons.

5 Spiky leaves across a chignon.

6 Flowers all over a helmet base.

7 Tiny bunches of flowers.

8 Feathers and flowers combined.

9 Fabric cut to imitate feathers.

10 One flower at back, one at side.

11 Forward pointing flower and feather trim.

12 Wear one, carry one.

13 Tiny flowers and bows scattered over hair.

14 Pre-pleated fabric made into flowers.

15 Ribbons and flowers.

16 Giant flowers in soft floppy fabrics.

Fashion Look

For a very dressed-up occasion, you can go to town on a headdress, adding feathers, flowers, lace and frills, as well as ribbons and bows. Wear with a stunning dress, trimmed in the same way, and create a dramatic and extravagant effect.

Feather and Flower Combs

Combs are one of the most effective ways of attaching a headdress to the hair. Not only do they grip all but the finest of hair but they also form good firm bases on which arrangements of flowers, leaves, ribbons, feathers and other decorations can be built.

Flowers and Bows

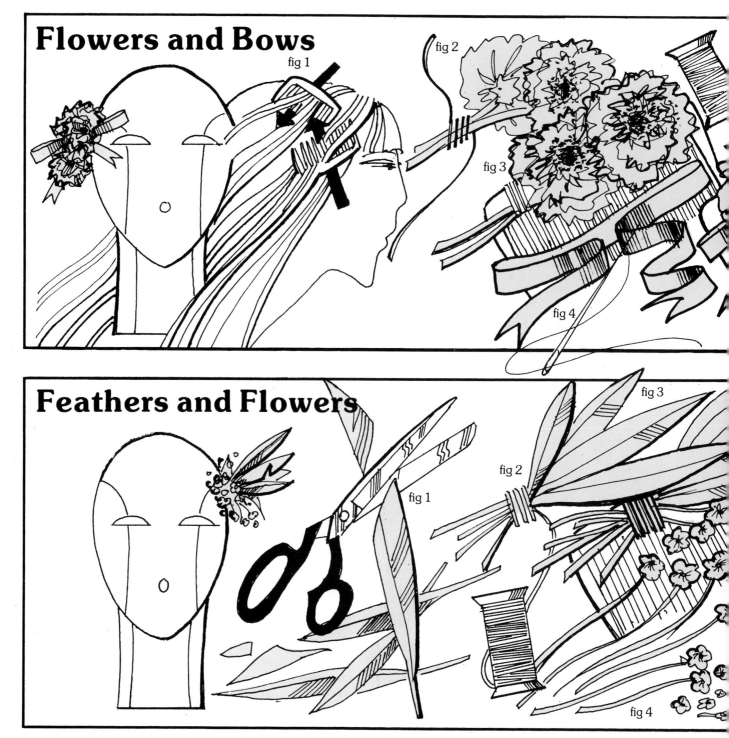

Feathers and Flowers

To make sure your comb grips tightly in the hair, first move it upwards through the hair. Then turn it towards the head, digging the teeth of the comb into the tangle thus created (fig 1). A comb pushed home in this way will support even a quite substantial decoration safely.

Flowers and Bows

fig 6

Materials
1 head comb
2 large artificial flowers with stalks
½m(½yd) of 1.3cm(½in) satin ribbon
1 bunch of tiny artificial flowers
1 reel fine wire

Method
1 Bind main flowers together with wire around the stalks (fig 2). Attach pair of flowers to comb by winding wire through teeth of comb and over flower stalks (fig 3).

2 Prepare a bow of satin ribbon (fig 4). Attach bow to comb with wire, placing it carefully between the blooms (fig 5).

3 Break up bunch of small flowers. Fill in gaps and hide wiring by glueing on small flower heads (fig 6).

Feathers and Flowers

fig 5

Materials
1 head comb
6 feathers with stiff shafts, such as pheasant, eagle or ostrich
2 bunches of tiny artificial flowers
   1 reel fine wire

Method
1 If necessary cut down or reshape the feathers by trimming their flights at top or bottom (fig 1). Bind them together by winding wire round shafts, arranging feathers so that they are placed at interesting angles, as opposed to lying parallel (fig 2). Attach group of feathers to comb by winding wire through the teeth of comb and over shafts of feathers (fig 3).

2 Break up bunches of flowers and wire individual specimens onto comb (fig 4). Fill in remaining gaps and hide wiring by glueing on small flower heads (fig 5).

More Decorative Combs

For elaborate dressed-up occasions you can really go to town and add lots
of different ingredients to a comb headdress, especially if your outfit is
classically simple enough to take it. Let the elements of the hair decoration
be as varied and complex as you like, and try using sharp, striking colours.
Here are two original and attractive ideas for comb decorations which can
easily be modified or adapted to your own requirements.

Soft Spotted Bow

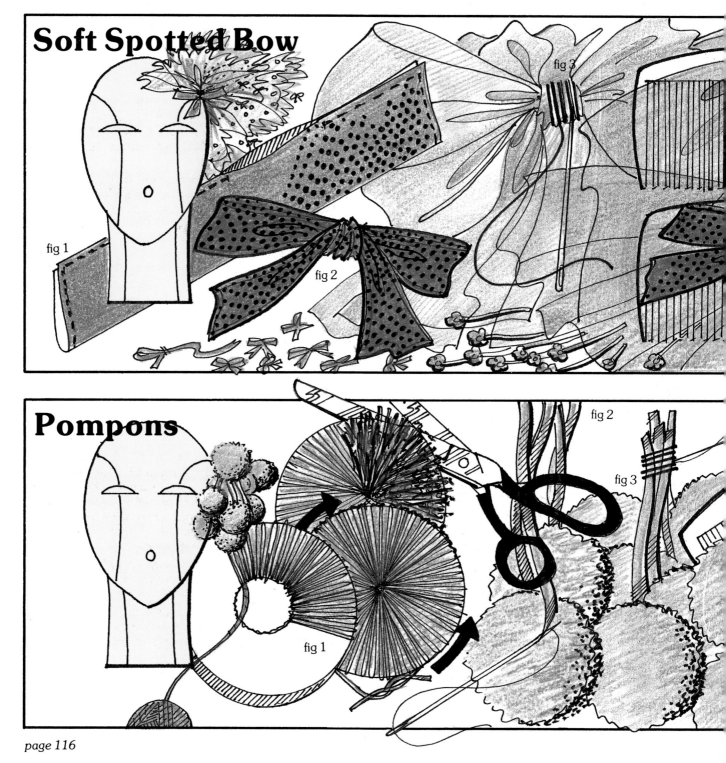

fig 1

fig 2

fig 3

Pompons

fig 1

fig 2

fig 3

Soft Spotted Bow Comb

Materials
1 head comb
½m(½yd) dotted voile
¾m(¾yd) millinery veiling
Selection of sequins
2 bunches tiny artificial flowers
1m(1yd) double-sided 0.6cm(¼in) satin ribbon
1 reel fine wire

Method
1 Cut strip of dotted voile ½m(½yd) long and 18cm(7in) long. Fold it in half lengthwise, right side to right side. Pin, and then machine stitch round edges, leaving a 5cm(2in) opening in centre (fig 1). Turn it through, slip stitch up opening, and then press. Tie into natural bow shape (fig 2).

2 Gather millinery veiling into an attractive mass by folding, gathering, oversewing and occasionally cutting some of the loops thus formed. Oversew veiling onto top of comb (fig 3).

3 Attach bow to veiling with several tacking stitches. Secure trim to comb by wrapping fine wire tightly and neatly round both (fig 4).

4 Prepare small bows and groups of ribbons from satin ribbon. Break up bunches of flowers, and glue these and ribbons onto comb to fill in gaps and to hide wiring and stitching (fig 5).

5 Decorate veiling by glueing sequins and flowers onto veiling dots, covering both sides of veiling at the same point, so as to avoid leaving unsightly glue marks underneath. Keep the decorations springy and not so heavy that they will pull the veiling down.

fig 4

fig 5

Pompons on Combs

Materials
1 head comb
3 or 4 ready-made feather pompons
1m(1yd) satin ribbon
or
3 or 4 knitting yarn pompons (ready-made or prepared at home from knitting yarn)
1m(1yd) plaited yarn

Method
1 If you choose feather pompons as the trim, buy these ready-made. Knitting yarn pompons can however be easily made at home. Prepare two card discs of 1.5cm(½in) to 6.5cm(2½in) diameter with circles cut in the middle. Wind yarn round and round discs placed together; tie centres, and then cut loops of yarn at edges to form pompon (fig 1). Trim to neaten edges. Repeat process for as many pompons as you need.

2 Prepare ribbon or braided yarn into different lengths from 4cm(1½in) to 9cm(3½in). Join ribbon/yarn ends to pompons by attaching them deep in pompon centres (fig 2).

3 Group pompons and join free ends of ribbons/yarn together by oversewing (fig 3). Attach decoration to comb by sewing oversewn ribbon/yarn ends to comb, so that group of pompons hangs from comb in an attractive arrangement (fig 4).

4 Prepare two tiny yarn pompons or small satin ribbon bows, and attach to decoration to mask the stitching on the comb (fig 5).

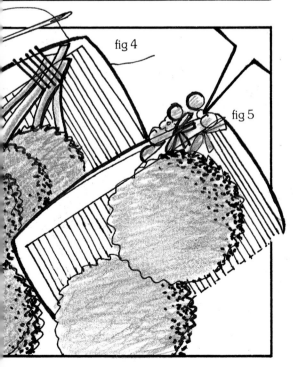

fig 4

fig 5

Men's Hats for Women

As with clothes, many of the hats that were once thought of as solely for the use of men, are now widely adopted by women. From flat caps to crash helmets, and trilbies to stetsons, men's hat styles have been transferred from use by one sex to acceptability by both; in reality 'unisex' is much more to do with women adopting men's fashions than free interchange of styles between men and women.

The type of man's hat that women like to wear tends to be of the sporty and casual kind, rather than the formal topper or bowler – the functional rather than the frivolous. Practical men's hats combine well with the workwear, sportswear and daywear now thought of as perfectly normal for women: boiler suits, track suits, overalls, anoraks, tweed jackets, trousers and waistcoats (and their equivalents in hats) all now form the basis of many women's wardrobes.

One of the most popular men's hats favoured by women is the flat cap. It is a perfect informal style, attractive and also useful for keeping rain out of the eyes and hair tucked away if wanted. It can be made up in a variety of fabrics, from tweeds to canvases, from the pattern on the next page. Other masculine styles to make yourself may be adapted from some of the patterns given earlier on. The Fatigue Cap (page 30–1) is itself an original man's USA army style, while a trilby can be constructed by adapting the cloche pattern (on page 28) to give a firmer base and a squarer crown. Soft summer cloches of the sunhat, rainhat and sporting varieties are worn by men and women alike, as are many knitted hats. If you like the idea of a man's straw style, it is quite simple to block one yourself. Choose a more masculine weave than you would for a feminine hat, a Panama or a tight, rough straw, and use the basic blocking techniques outlined on page 74 to create a successful tailored look.

Many ready-made men's hats, acquired from men's outfitters or hatters, can be adapted if desired. You may of course leave the trims as they are, but you can also easily alter them to give a more interesting and special, or even flamboyant effect, without losing their masculine quality. A decoration of a couple of fishing flies on a tweed or corduroy hat could be exaggerated by the addition of another half dozen for a more dashing look on a woman; add an extravagant brooch to a practical style to strike a nice contrast; or hang ribbons down the back of a boater for a more feminine touch.

As is shown on the page of fashion looks in this chapter, it is a good idea to make sure your clothes and your chosen men's hat style all work well together as an outfit. They will look much more effective and striking if you bear this in mind.

Flat Cap in Checked Tweed

This traditional man's flat cap looks very dashing on women
and is at its best worn with tweeds and Fair Isle sweaters in
the country. As with other soft hats made from flat patterns
(*see* pages 24–37) it can be made up in a variety of fabrics.
Try the stiffer cottons, such as canvas for summer, and wools
and tweeds for winter.

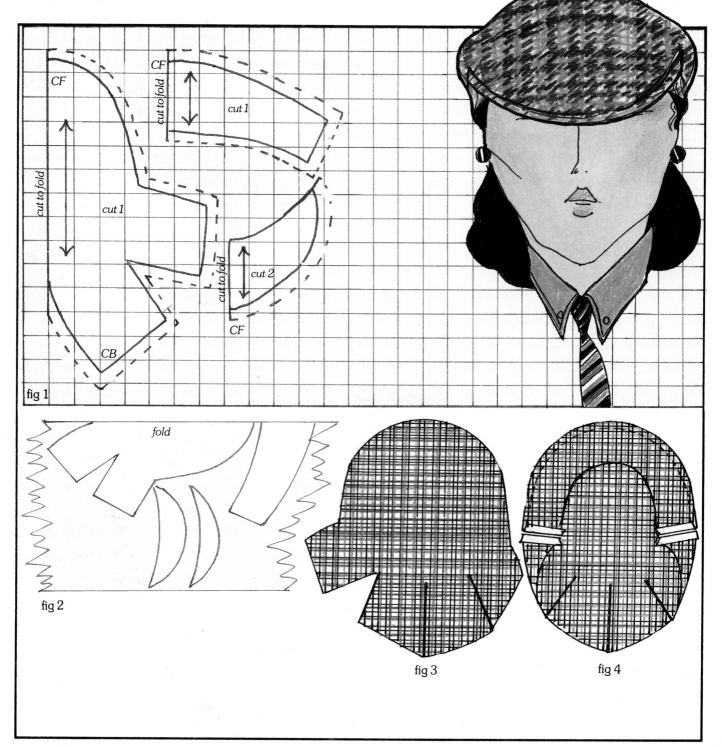

fig 1

CF

cut to fold

cut 1

cut 1

CB

CF

cut to fold

cut 1

cut 2

cut to fold

CF

fig 2

fold

fig 3

fig 4

Materials
½m(½yd) checked tweed
½m(½yd) lining
Buckram or cardboard for peak stiffener
Grosgrain ribbon for head fitting

Method
1 The pattern given is ¼ scale for a 57.2cm(22½in) head fitting. Scale up on to graph paper all measurements except seam allowances ×4 (fig 1). For other head sizes, *see* page 18.

2 Place scaled-up pattern on fabric following suggested lay, and cut out fabric and lining on the cross (fig 2).

3 Pin, tack and then machine darts in cap top as indicated on pattern (fig 3). Cut open darts and press. Stitch front band to cap top, right side to right side (fig 4).

4 Place two peaks together, right side to right side. Pin, tack and then machine round outer edge of peak. Clip and press seams open. Turn peak through and press again (fig 5). Insert peak stiffener into peak (fig 6). Top stitch edge of peak.

5 Clip peak turning every 1.3cm(½in) (fig 7). Pin, tack and then back stitch peak to front section of cap (fig 8).

6 Fold bottom edge of cap in around head fitting. Prepare curved grosgrain ribbon for a 57.2cm(22½in) head fitting. Pin and then slip stitch ribbon to inside the head fitting, hiding the front peak turnings (fig 9).

7 Prepare lining, if required, in same way as you have prepared cap top and front band. Pin, and then slip stitch lining into cap under grosgrain ribbon head fitting.

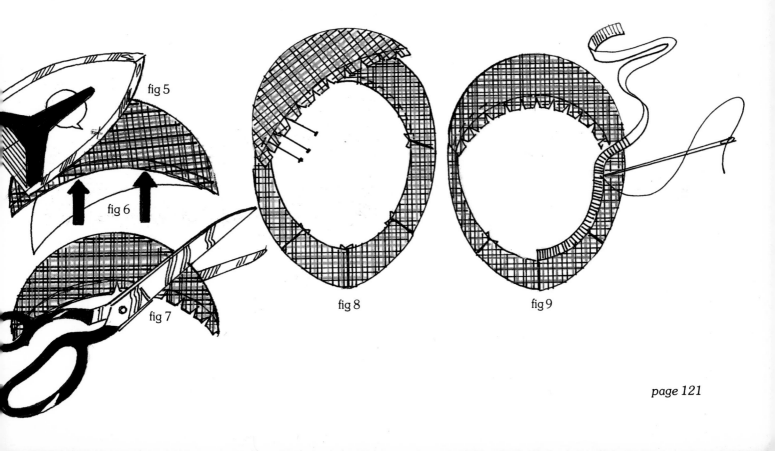

fig 5

fig 6

fig 7

fig 8

fig 9

Men's Hats for Women's Wear

Provided the hat suits you and makes you feel confident, and you combine it carefully with the right style of dress, many men's hat styles can look perfect with women's fashions. Co-ordinate the fabrics and colours of hat and outfit, choose the right occasion and you will be set to make a stunning impression.

1 Men's gabardine rainhats are as effective in keeping the rain off women as men, and they look very stylish with trench coats. Oilskins look good on all the family for water sports, as do bright plastics and cires.

2 A floppy cap that will earn a kid a sympathetic glance, this man's 1920s style will suit women as well.

3 Traditional fishing hats and tweed trilbies stitched all over and trimmed with fishing flies and feathers are perfect for country wear. Try them in corduroy or proofed cottons for inclement weather.

4 A man's bowler hat looks stunning and original on a woman, but wear it with strictly formal city clothes and the neatest of hair styles.

5 Harris tweed and other rough woollen cloches look good on both sexes. Wear them with sporty clothes, big overcoats or smart tweed suits.

6 'Resistance' style felt beret with obligatory stalk; French cyclists prefer black, parachutists red. Both colours look chic on a woman.

7 Ribbed, turned up rolls, worn low, make classic knitted hats for men and women. In jolly colours they make excellent earwarmers for children.

8 Summer cloches, in white, are perfect for cricketers and lady tennis players. For a child's sunhat try brighter colours as well as the traditional white.

9 You don't have to be a Hell's Angel to wear a leather cap!

10 Forage caps from the army surplus store: whether it is RAF, WRAF or WRACS, a military fashion for both men and women comes round every few years.

11 Crash helmets are legally necessary for all on motor bikes, but advisable for skateboard use as well!

12 Fair Isle knitted berets for both sides of the border look great on men, women and children alike.

13 A man's boater is smart for summer, but add some ribbons down the back for a fresh holiday feel.

14 Schoolboy caps are not as bad as you remember them. Wear them at the bowls club (or the rowing club for him).

15 Knitted jellybags are for genuine skiers but they will also keep both non-sporting men and women warm and cosy.

Fashion Looks

Men's traditional hat styles look good with all kinds of informal clothes, particularly sporty and casual looks. Match up fishing hats with green rain boots, stetsons with cowboy boots and so on.

Sportier country styles can be completed with correct accessories: traditional tweed trilby and fishing bag.

Man's flat cap looks great with soft easy jacket and old comfortable Fair Isle pullover.

Try a military beret with an army surplus fashion look — quilted over-jacket and anorak.

And a giant stetson to a fringed jacket and jeans and cowboy boots for an authentic western image.

Slick trilby for a slick double breasted pin-striped suit complete with tie and button hole.

Suppliers

Almost all the tools, equipment and materials needed to make or trim hats will be available at five and dime stores or at department stores. Most of the dress and furnishing fabrics mentioned can be purchased from your usual supplier, and trims (ribbons, flowers, sequins etc) from haberdashery stores or departments. Try wig stores for blocks and dolly heads. If you are planning to trim hats rather than to block your own, millinery departments in most stores offer a wide range of hats. They will also be able to advise you on specialist suppliers of millinery equipment if you are having difficulty in finding items. For knitting yarns visit your local stockists; they will be able to advise you on similar yarns if they cannot supply those suggested in the text. For information on local stockists of the Pingouin yarns mentioned in the knitting section contact: Promofil Corporation USA, 9179 Red Branch Road, Columbia, Maryland 21045.

Index